DOD

a novel by

Maurice Fickelson

translated by

J.A. Underwood

Calder & Boyars

First published in Great Britain 1972
by Calder & Boyars Ltd
18 Brewer Street London W1

Originally published in French as
Dod by Editions Bernard Grasset

ISBN 0 7145 0810 1

Printed in Great Britain by
Biddles Ltd, Guildford

DOD

Dod opens his eyes: he is in his bath. Next minute he is suffocating. His lips writhe hideously as he gasps for breath. He looks like a fish. And meanwhile a sound can be heard dying away, a sound like a whole ocean receding down the ages to its source. It is a nasty feeling to be a fish cast up on the shore without knowing how to breathe there. He beats at the sand with his caudal fin but this is useless; it brings him not a fraction of an inch nearer the irretrievable ocean. On the contrary his struggles, predictably enough, serve only to dig him into the ground. The more he thrashes about the deeper the crater becomes; the sky is already far off and still he is sinking, down among the shadows, the buried shells...To hibernate for a hundred thousand years. Perhaps by then the world will have changed, the waters again have covered the earth. A vague hope through the ebb and flow of the ice ages. But giant footsteps are jarring the beach. Mme Luffergal stoops over the crater, plunges in a naked arm, pulls the little fish out and tosses him into her basket. Now he is on the kitchen table. A bit thick, he thinks. He makes himself as sticky as he can, stickier than ever fish was before, but to no avail - blood itself could not adhere to green formica. This puts him off even so much as feebly flapping his tail. And so he stops thinking about this henceforth useless end of his body. He cuts himself off from it. He forgets it. Like a good, patient, thrifty little fish. Drawing himself in nicely. Having decided to wait it

5

is best to take up as little room as possible, the ideal of course being to occupy none at all. Now, though, brand-new lungs start to unfold and fill, a new era has begun, evolution has been complied with, the long night of geology can now be left behind. Deep in the alveoli, air and blood begin their communion.

Dod opens his eyes; he's in his bath, there is no doubt about that. A sound is fading away in the distance and the bathroom becomes a conch in which not the sea but a thousand nasty sharp little noises can be heard, tiny avalanches of sand grains, bones crumbling in tombs; or other sounds, muffled, intestinal, horribly close. Things creeping through tunnels with clenched jaws, blind greedy things nibbling their way forward. And at the centre of this riddled space, motionless, is Dod. He doesn't like it. He would rather be some-where else.

All the scattered noises have merged into the gnawing of one giant mouse. The beast hollows out it shole and immediately fills it with its bulk; the more it excavates the more it grows. It is wasting no time. Planets, comets, constellations, asteroids, all are swallowed up, the nebulae take flight but too late, this is the limit, this is the outer edge of the curve. The space-eating mouse has nothing left to gnaw. So it turns its attention to Dod. And the universe is filled with the beating of an enormous heart.

It is indeed a heart that the terrified Dod can hear beating. But not a mouse's heart. His own. His heart. Dod's heart. And how it's beating! It would beat no faster nor with more exaggerated force if it were trying to make up for lost eternity. Fruitless pursuit. Alas, he thinks. And still he feels the pounding of the blood in his ear-drums.

It is beating too fast, this heart. Dod cannot keep up, does not want to keep running, has never run,

cannot, does not want to be ill any more and have Dr.
Nauser's enormous face hover over him. He shuts
his eyes and plunges into a reddish obscurity. But
now the sound is coming back, a crowd of people is
closing round him, dragging him down dimly lit streets
towards the harbour...And suddenly sky and houses
start spinning round him, he feels himself falling, and
he grabs at the edges of the bath-tub with both hands.

The dizziness, the pressure on his face, the sensation
of being forever on the point of overbalancing, the
feeling of being ill at ease in space, the irresolute
manner in which lines and surfaces grope for the joints
between them, the obstinate way things have of sitting
a little to one side of where they are - Dod is quick to
recognize the initial symptoms of a migraine attack.
Permits himself a smile at his ridiculous fear. Settles
comfortably down behind the familiar affliction. The
natural explanation once found, it is easy to bear
patiently with the pain.
    Before long he notices his vision has contracted.
To the left there is nothing. To the left is a missing
space. Missing in all but the uneasy feeling caused
by its not being there. Dod, keeping his neck rigid,
watches this absence out of the corner of his eye.
Something is beginning to happen.
    At first it is no more than an imperceptible tension,
the effort a shadow might make to emerge from nothing-
ness. Then, the way a top which has been spun so
fast it appears still and colourless, its true state
suggested only by a faint blurredness of outline,
gradually loses momentum and its spinning motion
starts to become visible and colours to appear, in the
same way this numb area of Dod's field of vision, this
dead space to the left, this dead angle, so to speak,
this space, which a moment ago did not exist, now
comes to life, begins to move, quiver, glare...
    A phantasmagoric advertising display for the blind

7

is in crazy progress. It began with beautiful zigzags flashing across from left to right at regular intervals like on a television screen, promising a reasonable measure of pain and a certain amount of mental gratification. But once under way these immediately disappeared again, their message forgotten, chaos taking their place. There remains a kind of obscure groping sensation, shot through with occasional spasms, a few last ragged flashes of black neon, and then extinction. A return to the minimal conditions of existence? It could be, but for the persistent quivering of that blob of darkness to the left as it searches for a substance, a form, a shape to settle itself in - fixes on that of an amoeba, and immediately sprouts a coloured fringe which starts thrashing wildly. A vast, weightless, shadowy amoeba. By process of fission it becomes several amoebae. But these have no sooner separated than they merge again, reconstituting the original. This, to beat the problem of reproducing itself, tries another experiment - shrinks, compacts itself, pullulates on the spot. Gradually this repetition of blackness evokes a further space, deeper vistas of darkness. And the strange thing is the transparency, like the night of a rising moon, in which vague shapes are stirring, crowds, processions...Dod, a helpless witness of this weird and sickening spectacle, sees himself being flushed out of the refuge he had thought to find in his sufferings. The black blob is throbbing like a heart. With great, dull thuds that spill out whorls of dark, nocturnal music. In the intervals he can hear voices, snatches of song, stifled laughter, and simultaneously he is aware that it is he who is drawing these heavy, laboured breaths, he who is gasping, suffocating, his body that is racked with exhaustion after running for too long, his legs that hurt so much, and the people are moving aside for him, and he tells himself he has exceeded his strength but is at last going to be able to rest, he has only to

8

choose where to sink down. The pavement gave abruptly beneath his feet and he felt a kind of quick, powerful suction from below, coming just before the final leap of the ultimate echo.

A sound fading to nothing. Someone is moving away.

It is nine o'clock in the morning.

Dod opens his eyes and shivers. He must have fallen asleep in his bath and the water has gone cold. He presses his finger-tips to a painful throbbing in his left temple. Where is Mme Luffergal? He glances cautiously about him. Dizziness and nausea lurk in every corner of this blue-tiled cave. He could have fainted, possibly with fatal consequences, and if the woman does not turn up soon he is certainly going to catch a chill. He fancies he can already feel a tingling sensation in his nostrils and he begins to feel sorry for himself. How distressing to be at the whim of mercenary hands, dependent upon attentions that are not inspired by love. The thought brings tears to his eyes, and this, by sharpening the tingling sensation in his nostrils, immediately provokes a fresh wave of melancholy, exquisitely sweet. As a result the tears well up in his eyes and are on the point of brimming over in a flood of rare emotion when he sneezes. And fear suddenly materializes. Suppose Mme Luffergal doesn't come? Suppose she has broken her leg? Suppose she has met the little telegraph-boy who has handed her a telegram saying her daughter in Scotland is seriously ill? But it is extremely unlikely that Mme Luffergal has a daughter in Scotland, and difficult to imagine how she could even wobble on her formidable foundations, much less fall and break one of the columns that serve her as legs. The woman is nevertheless behaving in an irresponsible manner and Dod, the victim of her negligence, sternly disapproves.

He wonders whether he should not try to heave himself over the edge of the bath with his arms and then crawl out and across the room to his bed. But the effort required makes him lose heart. Besides, might he not risk falling on the tiled floor of the bathroom and hurting himself? An easier and wiser course would be to run a bit of hot water, although the tap is a long way off, right at the other end of the bath, and it would mean leaning forward very awkwardly to reach it. So he gives up and, seeing no other way out, sadly contemplates the paleness of his body beneath the water. His gaze lingering on his shrivelled penis he notices something greyish there, is intrigued - it is like a pad of old moss grown discoloured in the dark - but finds on closer attention that it is caused by a mass of tiny bubbles clinging to his pubic hair. Curious, he says to himself, and then the anguish returns.

But a door has just been shut. There is someone in the kitchen, banging things about. Dod heaves a deep sigh; he is filled with a rush of warm feelings towards Mme Luffergal whose tasks are so many and various. The self-denial that must be required, even when set against a generous renumeration, to take care of an invalid, someone who combines the helplessness of a child of tender years with the weight of a full-grown adult. Dod is ashamed of his ingratitude and of the wicked thoughts he was entertaining only a moment back.

Heavy foot-falls shake the delicate framework of the building and set the metal utensils gently tinkling on the kitchen walls. Mme Luffergal enters the bathroom. It is a small room and Dod immediately has her looming above him. She stands there for a moment, hands on hips, looking at him the way she would look at a potato that needed peeling, or a pile of dirty washing-up. Then she leans down, plunges a pair of enormous pink arms into the water, slides them under Dod's hips and thighs and with no apparent effort lifts him out. She lets him drip a bit before carrying him to his room.

Spread out on the bed is a thick bath towel. Mme Luffergal sets down her burden, straightens up again and contemplates Dod's naked body - it seems to shrink beneath her gaze - this time with the satisfaction of a woman who is inured to work and feels a certain pleasant impatience to begin. She covers his nakedness with the edges of the towel and with her huge, powerful fists starts to chafe and burn his skin. Showing, however, immense tact in the matter of drying his private parts. That done, she throws a tartan blanket over him and goes out to the kitchen to make the coffee.

The blanket is too short or has been carelessly arranged, or has possibly been placed sideways instead of lengthways; Dod notices that his feet are sticking out. He scrutinizes them from a distance. For a closer view of them he would have to push himself up with his elbows to a sitting position, then lean forward... Too much trouble.

Dod is lost in contemplation of his feet: the right stands proudly at the vertical while the left, whether from modesty or incompetence, leans inwards at an angle of approximately fifteen degrees. This is its natural position. Dod has no power to alter it, any more than he has to move his toes. But he says to himself this is just what he is going to try and do - move his toes. He scrutinizes them, checking the positions of the joints, And is already sorry. He wishes the idea had never occurred to him. Would like to look away. Call Mme Luffergal and ask her please to cover him up a bit better. He feels cold. No, of course not, his feet aren't cold, what a ridiculous idea. It's just that he doesn't want to see them any more. Doesn't like them. He is afraid. The pleasing tranquillity of the lower part of his body has given way to an unbearable feeling of tension. He feels almost faint when he

fancies he sees a gap between his left big toe and the
toe next to it which was not there before. As if an
eye were opening. This is so clearly a poor comparison
that it reassures him. Dod is quite prepared to stare
back at an eye regarding him from his foot and derive
a healthy amusement from it. The thing would be
preposterous but the event of no consequence; our
sober world is continually casting up a froth of equally
insignificant phenomena. What, on the other hand,
there would be no tolerating would be any alteration of
a man's living space by the improbable displacement
of a toe.

Mme Luffergal comes out of the kitchen. She pulls
back the blanket, picks Dod up in her arms and sits
him in the chair. She is going to dress him. This
she does like everything else - vigorously, nimbly,
with a certain peasant quality of movement and such
inexorable thoroughness that it never even occurs to
Dod to perform such possible but unthinkable actions
as buttoning his own shirt and trousers. Instead he
abides by what is expected of him: a vague physical
compliance. Powerless to bring about the slightest
change in his surroundings or in the course of events,
he contents himself with deriving from his observation
of them certain clues, and from their indeterminacy
certain omens. Thus, as Mme Luffergal reaches out
an arm towards the chair on which his clothes hang,
Dod has a fraction of a second before she completes
the movement - will she pick up his pants or his socks
first? - in which to augur the prospects, whether
favourable or unfavourable, of the coming day. Heads
or tails, odds or evens, pants or socks, this is his
first omen. There will be others in the hours ahead,
following the day's routine, to corroborate or modify
it, but none can invalidate the morning augury. That
is the game. It provides Dod with a certain transitory
excitement, some sad or happy thoughts, and the
occasional confusion of mind brought about by long

series. When the pants had come up nine days running
he had begun to wonder whether chance had not been
supplanted by some law. The very idea that Mme
Luffergal might have the power to decree a new law
had indeed given him something to think about. But
on the tenth day everything had reverted to indeterminacy

Dod is sitting by the window, gloomily observing the
red eye of the electric toaster. This morning the
omens were unfavourable. And the pain in his left
temple has dug itself in. A subtle and persistent
nausea is pinching at his nostrils and the idea of
eating fills him with repulsion. He even finds the
smell of the coffee irritating. When migraine takes
possession of a body it drives away everything that
might detract from its own jealous presence. It will
even go as far as to exile that body in silence and
darkness, forbidding it the least movement. Such is
the exclusive character of migraine. Dod wonders how
he can outwit its vigilant custody. Would it allow one
cup of coffee and one lightly, very lightly, buttered
round of toast? Not a question of being keen, no, nor
of really wanting it, not that, it would be more out of
duty, a kind of civility, something English, although in
England apparently they drink tea, and tea would
certainly be more digestible, but there is no tea here,
more's the pity, on the other hand there is toast,
toast is English too, and insubstantial, and digestible.
The red eye goes out. With a little click the toaster
half-ejects two rounds of toast which then sit there,
looking, thinks Dod, ridiculously pleased with themselves and with the progress of technology. And he
remembers the lovely fat farmhouse slices he used
to have as a child, and how the milk foamed in the
flowered bowls, etc. Having paid this tribute to
literature, he takes one of the rounds of toast and
proceeds to butter it carefully.

14

Dod pours himself another cup of coffee and lets his
gaze wander out of the window. The landscape of
concrete and greenery has dreamily dressed ranks.
Is this the same scene as he was looking at yesterday?
It seems familiar. Towards the top it has that stretch
of poplar-lined road which does not quite fit in, as
if it were a piece from another puzzle. A schoolboy
has just come into view there, dressed in one of those
black pinafores that schoolchildren do not wear any
more. He has a satchel on his back, his hands in his
pockets, and from time to time he is seen to kick a
pebble across the road, or smile at distant, carefree
recollections. He is so late already that it is really
not worth hurrying; in fact he even slows his pace.
He fancies he can recall some agreeable and tender
memory, but then the light changes and the thought is
lost. The child chuckles to himself. The tall poplars
suddenly begin to sway about - is it happiness? Dod
crumbles a piece of toast between his fingers, his
mind searching vaguely for an explanation. He is about
to give up, but then leans forward and takes a dictionary
from his desk. He opens it at random, eyes closed,
pokes a finger at the page, looks, finds the word
'pelorus', and is puzzled. Not knowing what to do with
it. 'Pelisse', a little higher up, possibly... Like the
black-pinafored schoolchildren used to wear... This
is a dead-end, but then right at the bottom of the page
is the word 'penitent'. The woman, kneeling among
her veils, is about to turn towards him a face which
he knows will be of exquisite beauty when Mme Luffergal
pushes back the chair and begins to clear the table.
Dod puts a hand to his temple; he suddenly feels very
ill and asks in a weak voice if she will be so good as
to open the window.

Mme Luffergal has wrapped the tartan blanket round
his knees. With eyes half-closed he offers his face to
the fresh air. Gradually his gaze becomes more

attentive as he searches for an imperceptible anomaly
in the landscape which has aroused his suspicions.
Before him stretch lawns and a quadruple row of trees
leading towards the central part of the park. On
either side of this tract of greenery and at right angles
to his building are two long blocks of five storeys each.
Since his chair has been placed slightly at an angle he
can see without bending forward the whole of the facade
of the right-hand block but only the far third of the
block on the left. His view extends to the line of
white buildings belonging to the New University, though
these are partly hidden by two of the fifteen-storey
tower-blocks recently erected on that side of the park.
A line of poplars in the left-hand corner indicates the
presence of a road, which is not visible from this
angle, or a river. The low, oval-shaped building half-
buried in russet foliage towards the middle of the park
houses the Cultural Centre, library and meeting-rooms.
If he bends forward Dod can see the whole of the facade
of the left-hand block and beyond that a number of other
blocks, the road that serves them, and the commercial
centre. If he turns his head through approximately one
hundred and twenty degrees he can see other, similar
buildings, the same road, known as the Avenue du 24-
Avril, and the playing-fields stretching away toward
the waste-ground which they will be building on too
before long.

A lingering mist softens the slanting beams of the
October sun. Everything seems to be in its place, yet
Dod remains sceptical.

His attention is suddenly attracted by a movement
on one of the paths to the Cultural Centre. A black
precession is leaving the building. Twenty people at
most, both men and women as far as it is possible to
judge from this distance, all dressed in dark clothes,
moving in an irregular formation with gaps of varying
sizes appearing between individuals. A row of trees
soon hides them all from view. But now, several

16

yards behind the rest of the company, a small figure
has appeared it is not a child - a twisted, hunch-backed
figure, hurrying to catch up with the others, his
jolting gait giving the impression of an irregularly
shaped object bouncing bumpily down a slope. Then he
too passes out of sight.

For several minutes Dod turns this vision over in
his mind. He senses that it is connected with other,
disparate elements, with that clock in the distance
striking an indeterminate hour, possibly the clock on
the University chapel, possibly farther off. Dod
thoughtfully strokes the blanket on his knees and wonders
why the summons of a solitary bell should so fill his
heart with fear and longing, and why the silence into
which it falls should be so deceptively similar to that
which greets you when something, you know not what,
wakes you up in the middle of the night.

It was indeed a nocturnal void through which he was
lazily, motionlessly rising, eyes closed, as a distant
clock struck the hour, eleven maybe, or midnight.
His legs felt cold. Yet his hand recognized the texture
of the blanket. He was suddenly aware that he was
lying fully dressed on a bed that was still made. Clocks
and belfries near and far, some deep-tone, some high,
rang out their warnings one by one. At each stroke,
as if from the vibrations, a fresh crack appeared in
his immobility. Shivers ran through his limbs. He
freed one hand and raised it to his eyes but could not
bring himself to open them; he was bothered by a dim,
fading image, or rather by the vaguely painful impression
it had left on him. It seemed, indistinctly, to be a face.

Dod let fall his hand and opened his eyes. The bells
had stopped ringing, but one last, infinitesimal vibration
lingered on and on in the silence.

Someone is talking to you and stops abruptly in the
middle of a sentence, looking as if he were somewhere
else; his mind is obviously not on you any more. You

17

try and attract his attention but he begins to bite his lip, clearly wondering what you are doing there and at a loss to understand your importunity. Finally he throws back his head and adopts a glazed look about the eyes to show what a nuisance you are being. In the same way Dod, while looking out of the window - what else can you do when you have a migraine attack? - as a clock struck eleven or noon, has lost contact with his surroundings. He is disconcerted and starts to fidget in his chair. His gaze goes straight past things, no longer able to focus on them. The landscape is coming apart before his eyes. Patches of white appear here and there.

It seems to Dod now as if this inadequately filled space is splitting in half. Or rather that foreign elements are attempting to enter through the gaps. Nature abhors a vacuum, he says to himself with some satisfaction; here is further proof. A woman comes into view round the corner of the right-hand building. She stops, puts down a heavy shopping-basket, picks it up again in the other hand and walks on. He tries to focus on her but it is no good; his painful efforts at concentration succeed only in keeping her at the edge of his field of vision, a blurred silhouette perpetually on the point of giving way to a tall, gaunt figure standing in the pouring rain by a white house with green shutters. This lady - who goes by the name of Mrs. Mabel Crocker Jones and is believed to have had a fairly rollicking youth - is wearing an old-fashioned, flounced dress and has just opened a large red umbrella above her head. Dod assumes she is there to make up for what is lacking in the woman with the shopping basket, but their imperfect register divides his attention and is exceedingly tiring, particularly as his memories of Mrs. Mabel Crocker-Jones elude him. In the end he wonders whether he is not confusing her with someone else. Finding it impossible to make out her features, he hurriedly adds a beribboned bonnet to her costume.

This does not help matters. Mrs. Mabel Crocker-Jones fades into the English countryside and the woman with the shopping-basket continues on her way beneath the large red umbrella. The result, for Dod, is a recrudescence of his headache. He closes his eyes and attempts at random to console himself with an axiom: All things in nature uphold and prove one another. Thus that worm which the blackbird on the lawn has just seized by one end and which is still holding fast to the earth by the other - not for long, the bird being as energetic as it is hungry - thus that worm, stretched for one glorious second to twice its normal length, proves the existence of both earth and blackbird. This act of philosophic charity once accomplished, it is free to continue in the dark intestines of the earth. But this is an almost ideal example. As far as Mrs. Mabel Crocker-Jones and the woman with the shopping-basket are concerned, although they may uphold one another it must be agreed that they are far from proving one another, tending, on the contrary, to be mutually exclusive, so obstinately do they attempt at one and the same moment to occupy the same particle of space. Dod gives them time to come to some agreement. When he re-opens his eyes Mrs. Mabel Crocker-Jones is back under the red umbrella and is not, thank God, carrying the shopping-basket. Matters, however, evolve further. The woman with the shopping-basket makes her ponderous way through more or less hypothetical zones of presence and, as she proceeds, Mrs. Mabel Crocker-Jones begins gradually to fade away and relinquish her space until, two-thirds of the way along the right-hand building, she is no more than an uneasy feeling, a yearning, a memory or presentiment of a rainy morning in Hampshire by a white house with beautiful green shutters.

Dod turns to look at other parts of the landscape and finds everywhere the same sinister skirmishing between bodies that fail to occupy their proper space and disturbing, allusive, inconstant forms that cunningly evade too close an attention. And now the network of paths criss-crossing the park and disappearing into the distance gives way to a complex suburban traffic system complete with motorway, access roads and multi-level interchanges. Chrome and enamel cars, the epitome of speed and comfort, flash past through shafts of light. The presence of the city can be sensed nearby. In an open convertible, driven by a man whose face cannot be seen but who is known to be a young and go-ahead industrialist sits a very beautiful woman, her blonde hair flying in the breeze. Dod, without interrupting his observation of the park, has taken the wheel and is speeding towards the city. The blonde woman is beside him. He tries out of the corner of his eye to distinguish her profile. He is on the point of recognizing her and remembering her name when a window in the right-hand building swings open and a flash of reflected sunlight dazzles him painfully. He calls weakly for Mme Luffergal to bring him a basin, he would feel so much better if he could vomit. But there is not a sound. Mme Luffergal has gone out again.

Dod slowly passes his hand over the tartan blanket wrapped round his knees. He thinks of a chameleon landing on a plaid and starts to laugh, his heart suddenly filled with despair.

The door moves slightly just as the schoolgirl's head
comes into view. Her face is an indistinct blotch amid
a tousled mass of hair - and it is strange, says Dod
to himself, that the face should be so indistinct when
it has the daylight full on it, a late afternoon light
certainly, and filtered through all the fogs of November,
but quite adequate, however dull, although after
travelling the whole length of the room...and he knows,
does he not, how far it is to the door? Yes, he knows,
and he realizes that the grey light of a late afternoon
in November, exhausted after travelling the whole
length of the room, is incapable of capturing the tiny
face which has appeared round the half-open door, and
the confusion of whose features resolves itself, on
closer examination, into an astonishing mobility of
expression. Suddenly the wandering eyes fix on Dod;
the blurred face condenses, sets, establishes itself
in the private time-scale of the room. The schoolgirl
watches as Dod tries to force himself to smile,
mechanically hoists the blanket up over his legs,
searches for something to say and fails to find it. Can
she see he is afraid? What actually does she see?
Her unblinking eyes reflect only objects. And the use
she will put them to is entirely unpredictable - the
most he can hope for is a measure of discretion in
her wilfulness. He is at her mercy.

The schoolgirl pushes open the door and enters the
room; she is clad in blue denim, leather and cartridge
paper, the large T-square sticking up at an angle of

approximately forty-five degrees. She takes a few
paces forward and stops, her eyes still on Dod, the
immobile, captive, lowly Dod who has at last managed
a smile. Then she too consents to smile and unhurriedly
takes possession of the premises. She deposits her
accoutrements on the table, first the cartridge paper
and the large T-square, then the leather brief-case
stuffed with books. She now has her arms free. Dod,
aware of and ashamed of his childishness - but what
else can he do? - begins talking furiously. Talking to
flatter, restrain, deflect or bewitch the powers of evil
yet again, or at least make an attempt. He begins
questioning her about school without stopping to wonder
at the stupidity of his questions. Is not stupidity the
best protection? School, the teachers, her girl-friends,
termly exams...If prayers have to have words at least
one should not worry what they mean. It is even, says
Dod to himself between two questions, a matter of
certainty that meaningful words have no chance of
reaching the godhead, this being the object of prayer -
not the absurd design of making oneself understood.
The schoolgirl answers in haughty, off-hand mono-
syllables. She is content for the time being to follow
her exploring hands, opening Dod's books, picking up
Dod's pen, Dod's pipe, sniffing it disgustedly. She
fiddles with the lighter, tries to make it work, can't,
drops it, picks it up, examines it again, and then turns
round.

'How does this work?' she asks.

Dod, giving thanks, lights the flame and explains.
When she has lit the flame five or six times herself
she loses interest in the lighter.

Then, possibly by association of ideas, she asks,
'What would you do if the building caught fire?'

Dod's heart starts to beat faster. The schoolgirl
leans forward, her large eyes soaking up what is left
of the wan light. The room is beginning to get dark.
She thumbs the lighter again and Dod can see the double

flame dancing in her steady eyes. One day, some day, he is going to find gathered at his bedside all the powers whose impassive circlings, sly approaches or abrupt about-faces he has studied with apprehension for so long - and there will be no more need then for him to puzzle over their visitations, their bustle or their silence, their incomprehensible evolutions - some day he will find them bending over him and he will see, dancing in their eyes, this glimmer of dangerous gaiety.

But the schoolgirl has already gone. Away in a dark corner of the room a pile of books collapses to the floor. She comes back towards him.

She asks, 'Can you really not walk - not at all?' She reflects for a moment before concluding: 'You're an invalid. That's sad.'

Dod cannot see her. She is behind him, behind the chair with the big wheels and the adjustable back in which he spends most of his time, and in which he is at the moment reclining. The little voice is whispering softly in his ear.

'You're an invalid. You're unhappy. But I love you and I'm going to look after you and take care of you. I'll be your little nurse. Then you won't be unhappy any more.'

The room is slowly revolving. The window has disappeared. The big wheels turn without a sound. They are always kept well oiled. The schoolgirl is humming something vaguely like a lullaby. Dod, his neck tensed, watches with terror the moving walls of this room he believed faithful to his own immobility.

'Stop it,' he says weakly.

And this plaintive cry, uttered without hope, miraculously works - or is it just a coincidence? Because one cannot be too careful when drawing connections between cause and effect, and how could such a pitiful exorcism have disarmed the powers of vertigo? Dod, now facing the open door, relishes

23

this moment of respite. It would be vain to hope for more. And indeed the chair once more begins to move with disturbing, inexorable slowness before again coming to a halt. Dod is out on the landing, bathed in the hospital light which is thrown up by the pane of frosted glass below. A breeze, wafted up from the abyss of the lower storeys, touches his brow. The schoolgirl is invisible. She is speaking to him: 'I'm your little nurse. I can do anything I like with you. You'll have to be good because...I don't like patients who aren't good and I want to like you very much. You must be absolutely obedient and listen to what I say. Because otherwise...'

The banister gives a sudden leap towards him and then slips away to the left and Dod sees the stone steps, sees space yawn open and the steps plummet into the void, witnessing their motionless fall before closing his eyes and sinking back in his chair with the schoolgirl's thin voice piping in his ear: 'What would you do if I pushed you down the stairs? You'd fall right down to the bottom and you'd kill yourself - it's a cert. You can't stop me pushing you. I will if I want to. I'll say it was an accident. I'll be very sad because I love you very much. So you have to love me too. You have to do what I say. Say you'll do what I say. Promise?'

Dod promises. Again space whirls around him before resuming the dull, reassuring shape of his room. Dod sees the schoolgirl standing there before him, smiling, strange as it may seem, shyly at him. He notices an ink stain on her nose, a very small blue ink stain, and he is overwhelmed with pity at seeing her suddenly vulnerable. There is no getting away, he tells himself, from the world's limitless distress.

She takes a step backwards, then another... She walks backwards all the way to the table where she left her things and waits there hesitantly, eyes downcast. At last, in a voice that is not her own, she says: 'I have to go now. I'm late.'

She glances quickly at Dod, sees him weakened with pity and tenderness, defenceless, and abruptly resumes her power.

'I'll be back tomorrow. I'll come and see you every day.'

Inflexible beneath her carapace of leather and cartridge paper, the large T-square poised threateningly, she subjects him to a stern appraisal, watching for the sign, the pretext for pouncing on him once again. Dod is careful to make no movement. With his eyes he signals his acquiescence, his willingness to be good, his utter dependence. But why this unexpected look of terror on the schoolgirl's face? She has thrown back her head and is looking at the ceiling. God, how stupid she looks with her mouth open like that! Then he understands; he too has heard the blows moving across the ceiling above them, the muffled yet precise tapping, has recognized the familiar, inexorable rhythm.

'It's old Lousine,' whispers the schoolgirl. 'It's old Lousine with her walking-stick.'

And Dod wonders what hierarchy can govern the Powers - for is it not conceivable that they obey rules and are ordered by laws as rigorous as their world is more complex than our own? And were this complexity no more than the fruit of our incomprehension, of our inability to perceive their nature, it would none the less find expression in an apparent incoherence in their manifestations. It is in any case obvious, as Dod notes with a certain feeling of pleasure, that old Lousine occupies a position of some eminence in that hierarchy, judging from the terror of this schoolgirl who now turns suddenly to the door - though the tapping has ceased - bumps into Mme Arthème on her way out, apologizes and is gone.

'That little girl's a nuisance,' announces Mme Arthème, shutting the door. 'Why can't you tell her to leave you alone? She bothers you.'

Dod makes a vague gesture of denial, comes up

25

against Mme Arthème's glare, and mutters, 'She doesn't bother me much.'

'Why are you sitting in the dark?'

She turns on the light, goes over to the window and draws the curtains. She takes off her raincoat and hangs it carefully over the back of a chair. The room arranges itself round her, flattens itself against the walls, makes way for her. Inanimate objects resume their insignificance as with precise, conclusive gestures she establishes her reign of terror. Snapping threads wherever she goes. Dod follows her movements, their geometry holding no mystery for him. Did she not haunt the nights of his childhood, hovering through his sleepless hours in the dim glow of the night-light? Her shadow would be on him even before he was aware of it, and he would sink into sleep in the very moment she emerged from the silence and the fear, her tall figure dispensing oblivion, before whom things were still.

'Can you explain,' she asks, 'why Mme Luffergal is not here yet? I like you to have an early supper and she has my instructions to that effect. An early supper and early to bed, that's what you need. The nights are never long enough for you.'

After pausing for a reply which Dod feels incapable of giving her, she continues: 'A number of other example of carelessness have come to my attention. Mme Luffergal is an extremely devoted and competent woman an excellent cook beyond any doubt and a person for whom I have a very high regard. I acknowledge that she keeps your room scrupulously clean at all times. But there are occasions when she takes things a little too much for granted. It is my opinion she should buck up her ideas about what is entailed in looking after an invalid. You, poor boy, can exercise no authority and unfortunately it is difficult for me to be here all the time.'

'Mme Luffergal is very good to me,' he says guarded

26

The nurse gives a shrug - 'It's not goodness you need, it's looking after' - and disappears into the kitchen.

The kitchen and bathroom together form a block which is situated on the right looking towards the window and takes up two-thirds of the length of the room. The visitor thus first enters a sort of corridor which is fairly dark, passing successively the door to the kitchen and the door to the bathroom before coming to the largest and best lit part of the room, containing a couch, an armchair, a desk, a book-case and the little table where Dod has his meals and which is usually placed by the window. This living-space, known as a studio - and repeated on all ten floors of the building at the corners, the rest being made up of four- or five-roomed flats - continues around the end of the bathroom, forming a recess or alcove which contains Dod's bed.

Faint clattering noises, the tinkle of glass and metal, rather like pin-points of light, flashes of crystal in a cave, sparks glinting through the foggy buzz of the sirens of fatigue, the descending scale of water coming to the boil - Dod is listening vaguely to the sounds coming from the kitchen when the figure of Mme Arthème suddenly looms above him. He did not see her coming. There is always something abrupt about Mme Arthème's appearances. She is holding up at eye-level a hypodermic syringe, her thumb resting on the head of the plunger. Dod concentrates his gaze on the needle but cannot distinguish the point - not until it spurts out a little jet of liquid, proving that the syringe works. Then, quite naturally, acting purely on long-established reflexes, he performs the required sequence of movements, raising himself slightly out of the chair and slipping down his pyjama trousers under the blanket. As the large, impassive, ageless face bends down towards him, Dod closes his eyes.

27

Dr. Nauser's face was hovering over him. He knew it
by the big nose, the drooping eyelids, the way all the
features were drawn downwards, and by that look of
having always known things about you which, however
hard you tried, you would never find out for yourself.

Dod let fall his hand and opened his eyes. Dr.
Nauser vanished just as he was on the point of saying,
'Well, my boy, here you are again.' Then he would
have turned towards the back of the room where Dod's
parents stood motionless, shoulder to shoulder. And
he would have continued: 'Take him home and put him
to bed. I'll call in and see him in the morning. The
blighter's made me miss the end of the first act.'

Dod is laughing quietly - possibly Dr. Nauser did
call next day but he had already gone from that house
and that town - when another image materializes out
of his memory and cuts short his laugh: in that dusty
room in the Municipal Theatre, probably the manager's
office, where he had regained consciousness, a young
woman dressed in jewels and transparent veils was
standing by the door. She had just come in. Her face
was drawn with a tiredness the make-up could no
longer conceal, and she was watching him with a look
of cool curiosity. Dod, frightened at seeing her so
close and disturbed by her nakedness, had sought a
desperate refuge in incomprehension, while his parents,
still standing shoulder to shoulder and holding hands,
had turned with incredible slowness towards the
apparition. At that moment Dr. Nauser had stood up

28

and, reaching the door in a few strides, as it were spirited the young woman away. In an obscenely sugary tone of voice he had said, 'This blighter nearly ruined the show. Fortunately we're rid of him now.' Dod had noticed then that Olivier was there too, and that he was biting his nails the way he always did when he had something on his mind.

Dod's parents are there, sitting side by side looking old and sad. They have the same tired expression on their faces, and there is a certain vague resemblance between them which comes from their wearing identical apparel. Although the only lamp is shining almost directly on them, their faces are somehow still partially in shadow. They are dressed in black. They do not move. They are watching over their sleeping son. In fact he has been awake for several minutes already, but has been careful to preserve this appearance of sleep which is his protection. A smell of vegetable soup hangs on the air and a series of emphatic sounds is coming from the kitchen: Mme Luffergal has arrived. Dod's parents are sitting very straight in their chairs, waiting, patient and sad: Dod opens his eyes and his father begins to speak:

'Son, your mother and I are here because we are worried. It's a long and tiring journey for such as no longer enjoy the vigour of their youth. For you we have left the familiar surroundings in which we expect to see out our days and in which we had hoped to have you with us, left the little town which is as dear to our hearts as it is to your own, which knew you as a child scampering on restless legs down its ill-paved streets, and later knew your troubled adolescence. You do still remember it, don't you? - the cool shade of the old walls in the heat of summer? That place, so full of memories, we have now temporarily left behind. It's hard to break habits at our age, but how can we

30

enjoy the peace and repose earned by years of toil when we are in such torment of spirit on your account?'

His father falls silent and his mother begins to speak.

'You cause us a great deal of anxiety, my son. We often speak of you back at home, wondering what you are doing and how you are getting on and whether there isn't anything you want. We are never at peace. Mme Arthème is a trustworthy soul, but who can know better than your mother how to take care of you? I brought you into the world, I gave you life, and ever since that day I have fought to preserve it.'

She falls silent, nodding her head. His father resumes.

'It is several weeks now since you left us, perhaps several months. We bowed to your wish, and although it seemed to us to be against your interests you must in fairness admit that we placed no obstacles in your way. Doubtless you need not have gone so far away to complete your studies, doubtless you ought to have taken into account our sorrow and affliction and the little time left to us on this earth. But you are our only son and we have always granted your every whim.'

Then it was his mother speaking.

'We do not reproach you for anything,' she says. 'You are our only son and we want you to be happy. Perhaps you do not realize what we have been through. You are still too young to understand. We could have been so happy there, the three of us, in that little town which is as dear to our hearts as it is to your own. The chrysanthemums have been lovelier than ever this year.'

She falls silent and his father speaks.

'We have always known you to be a respectful and affectionate son. Our love for you leaves us no room to doubt the love you have for us, a love we have nourished with our care, our sacrifices and our trust.

Didn't we bring you up according to the latest methods
of child-rearing despite our quite legitimate reservation
and the prejudices natural to an older generation? But
your letters are few and far between and they tell us
little. The reluctance you show in writing to us only
serves to increase our apprehension.'

'We are staying at the Excelsior Hotel,' says his
mother. Then again her voice glides to the surface of
the silence.

'No one comes to see us any more. Our friends are
all very old or sick or crippled, and some have already
departed this life. And we ourselves are too concerned
about you. We talk about you far into the night, for we
are unable to sleep. We wander like two lost souls in
travail through that huge empty house among the souvenir
and the photographs. Léone, our faithful maid, has
become more gloomy daily since you left.'

She sighs and nods her head. His father goes on.

'Why be so obstinate, son? We are your parents and
we only want you to be happy. Here where you have
chosen to live, in this city of inhuman size, you will
never be anything but an exile. Here no one seems to
be at home. The instability of these folk alarms me,
and I believe they are consumed by a secret fear.
Even their sadness is not like ours.'

His father falls silent and Dod can hear his mother
murmuring indistinguishable words. She sighs and
again the silence returns, broken only by his father's
congested breathing. The kitchen door opens. Smells,
sounds and colours accompany Mme Luffergal into the
room.

She rolls the little table with its steaming bowl of
soup over to Dod's chair. Then she straightens up,
hands on hips, mouth slightly open. A thread of saliva
trembles between her fat and quivering lips. Even
standing still she is surrounded by a sort of rustling,
a crackling of invisible sparks, a whirr of static.
When she moves it is in a kind of coloured mist, shot

through with fleeting glimmers and unexpected
flashes of light.

Dod's mother, who has dozed off, now wakes up,
moans, and finally becomes intelligible: 'Eat, my little
one, eat.'

And his father says, 'You must eat, son. Got to get
your strength back.'

Mme Luffergal's red bust is blazing before Dod's
eyes. His mother half-rises and begins to approach,
taking tiny steps and pulling her chair along with her.
It takes her some time to cover the short distance
separating her from her son for she is an old woman
and her legs are stiff. But she is coming; a careful
look is enough to note the progress she is making.
Suddenly Dod sees her standing over him with a spoonful of soup in her steady hand. She lifts it to her lips
and carefully blows the wreath of steam off it before
taking a swift, cursory taste - barely touching the edge
of the spoon in order to suck up a little bit of liquid,
so expertly was it done. Satisfied, she says, 'Eat up,
my child...'

His father rises to his feet and takes a few hesitant
steps across the room. He mutters absent-mindedly,
'Must eat,' and then is lost in shadow. A droning
noise is escaping from Mme Luffergal's lips. She has
begun to hum, with her eyes half-closed. Just as Dod
swallows the first spoonful of soup a series of dull
thuds makes the ceiling vibrate, letting him know old
Lousine is on the move. He can still hear his father's
voice from the other end of the room.

'You must eat,' he is saying.

A LETTER FROM OLIVIER

High Wycombe, Saturday 3 a.m.

Dod old friend,
I'm leaving in the morning and this letter, if I ever
send it, will reach you after I'm back. But I can't get
to sleep and I've got to talk to someone - Bob's gone
to bed. Anyway, talking to Bob...I can just see him,
putting his head on one shoulder and half-closing his
eyes: I'd no idea you were so romantic, Olivier. I
admire you, I really do. But it's late and we're both
pretty tired, aren't we? - You know Bob. Not that he
isn't a marvellous chap, don't get me wrong. I worship
him. But when I think he might never have invited me
to High Wycombe...Might things then, for such an
incredibly absurd reason, have gone differently? I
can't believe that. How can I accept that my whole
life, my salvation, my very raison d'être are dependent
on an inspiration of Bob's? It's ridiculous. No,
chance can have had nothing to do with it. It was all
decreed in advance, written in the stars, inevitable.
You'll have to decide for yourself, old man, because
I've gone right off my rocker. It's just happened and
it's marvellous. Unbearable, too. Like feeling the
ground give way under your feet, completely and utterly
and being whisked away like a straw in the wind...
Maybe you've already guessed - or maybe you haven't.
Would you ever have thought that I - sane, rational,
wise, cautious Olivier - would one day, one evening,
not just fall in but be totally swallowed up by love at
first sight? Thursday evening, to be exact, at the
Arts Theatre - and I'm not going to tell you about the

34

play. Bob and I had noticed Alwyn Jones sitting a few
rows in front of us - Alwyn's the chap I met last year
at Bob's place and who has a great-uncle who knows
you or anyway knew you apparently when you were
small and used to spend holidays in Hampshire - Redstone, I think his name is. He turned round and waved
to us, and then the girl sitting beside him turned round
too and Bob told me she was called Myra and that she
was a distant cousin of Alwyn's. After the show we all
met in the Salisbury.

Notice, by the way, that it's once again the theatre,
though this time it's my turn, that provides the 'scene
of the crash' - I'm thinking of that strange evening at
the Municipal Theatre. I'm sorry, it's my excitement
and ecstasy talking, but if the lightning struck at least
it didn't root me to the spot. And it hasn't just left
me with the memory of an illusion walking across a
stage but with a real being, more real than the world
itself...I'm sorry, I know the day will come when we'll
be puffing along behind you again, you old rogue. Do
you remember what you used to say: The way to God is
through movement, not through immobility; competition,
not contemplation.

I think it was at the precise moment when we came
out of the Salisbury that I knew with sober certainty
that Myra and I were bound together for ever and ever.
In the street the fog swallowed us up and she took my
arm.

I nearly forgot - it's not the most important thing
but it's certainly the oddest - Dr. Nauser's in London.
I caught sight of him sitting in a corner of the Salisbury,
apparently taking his usual secret delight in the foibles
of the poor mortals scuttling about before him. I don't
think he recognized me.

Next day, yesterday evening that is - no, last night,
it's hardly two hours since I left her - we all met again
at Alwyn's place at Marlow for the traditional Friday
night party, but I won't tell you about it because I don't

remember a thing. I was alone with her, the rest was mere shadow and confusion, a deathly cold gripping me every time she took her eyes off me.

What else is there to tell you? We're going to write to each other and I'll be coming back to High Wycombe at Christmas. If I can live till then.

See you soon,

Olivier.

'The last time we were in Hampshire...You were nine.
Life was still good to us then. We had a very pretty
white house with green shutters. It wasn't perhaps
the best sort of house for such a rainy climate, and it
rained more or less every summer. It was the rain
made your father grow tired of the place. And even
when the weather was fine he would still be gloomy;
one sensed he had something on his mind, I don't know
what it was. He's a good man and a kind one but he's
becoming difficult in his old age. One day he bought
the house in the South of France and we never went
back to Hampshire again.'

'Wasn't our next-door neighbour a Mrs. Mabel
Crocker-Jones?' asks Dod casually.

'Wherever did you get that from? I never knew
anyone by that name. Our only neighbour was Captain
Redstone, a dreadful man. He used to devote his
evenings to chemical experiments and he twice set fire
to his house. And bless me if he didn't come over one
day and tell me you'd been marked out by some sign or
other and that only an...initiate such as himself could
take your education in hand. I threw him out of the
house. He went off muttering dark threats and talking
about wasted opportunities and coming to a sticky end...
The man was mad.'

She broods bitterly for a moment and then her face
softens once more.

'The garden was lovely,' she says. 'I've never had
such beautiful flowers.'

She sighs and adjusts Dod's blanket. He would very much like to sit up a little higher in his chair but if he asks he will only be told that he is much better off the way he is, that otherwise there is a risk of his getting too tired... So he abandons the idea.

His mother's lips are moving and soon she can be heard saying: 'So your friend Olivier is in England. In November, for goodness' sake. He's an odd, uncommunicative, immoderate sort of boy, never could keep still - and I remember one occasion when he almost got himself expelled from Le Bocage School for some prank or other. Perhaps he's changed. At any rate I always found it hard to understand why you were friends. You were so different, the two of you.'

There are lights on in several windows in the buildings opposite and Dod becomes aware that night is falling. Then he hears the door opening. His mother turns her head and her face brightens.

'And who is this pretty little girl who's come to see us? Come here, child, don't be afraid. You're surely not frightened of me, are you? I'm Dod's mummy.'

The schoolgirl advances into the room taking small, cautious steps ready to flee at the first suspicious sign. And yet it is not Dod's mother she has her eye on but Dod, as if the danger could only come from him. She stops; without taking her eyes off him she says, 'Good evening, madame.'

It is clear that as far as she is concerned the presence of Dod's mother has altered the normal properties of the room and its occupant, and that she is debating with herself whether or not the change is for the good. Dod notices the extreme degree of concentration evident not merely in her face but in her whole body, as if she had just increased its weight in order to balance that of the intruder, at whom she now darts a furtive glance, followed by a smile of assent. She has received the answer to her question. And now his mother and the schoolgirl are both smiling at each other

38

'How nice of you to come and see my big boy,' says
his mother.

'He gets bored all by himself,' says the schoolgirl.
'I look after him. I don't always have the time, though.'

Dod becomes aware that two masses have just united
and brought about a change in the gravitational field
affecting the lighting, the shape and even the dimensions
of the room. The sudden increase in body-weight
presses him against his chair. His mother turns
towards him.

'What a delightful little friend you have,' she says.
But her smile becomes fixed and then gradually disappears. She stares at Dod's feet for ten seconds or
more without moving, showing by her posture and her
expression how deeply she is both surprised and shocked.
At last she murmurs, 'Unbelievable. Such thoughtless-
ness! And I've only just this minute noticed.'

Then, turning to the schoolgirl: 'Fancy putting shoes
on a boy who isn't going out and then leaving him like
that all the afternoon, perhaps all day - I'm sure the
shoes were put on this morning - in such discomfort,
and he says nothing, the poor boy, he dares say nothing,
he's much too shy to say anything at all. Whatever
does this Mme Luffergal think she's doing!'

'I don't like Mme Luffergal,' says the schoolgirl.

But his mother is already attacking one of the shoe-
laces. Without a moment's hesitation the schoolgirl
seizes his other foot. Dod wants to tell them he's
quite all right, they needn't bother, but one look at
their two heads, one fair and one grey, bending
together over his feet, persuades him to keep his
mouth shut. He sinks down in his chair and lets them
busy themselves with his extremities.

The schoolgirl stands up, brandishing a shoe.

'How clever your little friend is,' says his mother.
'So nimble. My old fingers aren't half as quick. I
can't think how Mme Luffergal tied this knot, you know,
but I'm sure I can't undo it.'

'I'm very good at undoing knots,' says the schoolgirl.
'Can I have a go?'

His mother stands aside and it is quite marvellous
to see the child untangle the knot in the twinkling of an
eye, loosen the lace methodically from top to bottom,
effortlessly draw off the shoe, pick up the other one
from the floor beside her and carry them both over
to the wardrobe and put them away, not without first
fitting them carefully with their shoe-trees. Back she
comes with his slippers and, kneeling down, puts them
on Dod's feet.

'A really domesticated little woman,' says his
mother. 'A proper little angel. Isn't Dod a lucky man?'

The schoolgirl lowers her eyes.

'I like looking after him very much,' she says.
'He's so nice. And it's very sad that he can't walk.'

His mother sighs and says something which is
incomprehensible. The schoolgirl takes no notice.

'I'm going to be a nurse when I grow up. I'll look
after people who are ill. I'll give them injections.'

'Oh, did you hear that!' says his mother, clapping
her hands together. She tries to catch Dod's eye; she
would like him to share her enthusiasm.

The schoolgirl attempts to assume a look of puzzlement as she says, 'I keep wondering whether he used
to be able to walk when he was little.'

'He began walking very late,' says his mother.
'Not until sixteen months.'

'It's better when children don't start walking too
soon.'

His mother and the schoolgirl both agree: walking
too soon deforms children's legs. Dod has a fine pair
of legs, lovely and straight. They examine them.
Touch them. Dod tells himself he can feel nothing.
But he looks away. There are lights on in at least
half the windows in the buildings opposite now. The
room seems suddenly much darker.

...He can no longer see anyone and he begins to worry. Did he doze off? Did they leave without him noticing? Perhaps it's later than he thought. But then he hears them whispering behind him. He catches a stifled laugh and wonders vaguely whether it is his mother or whether it is the schoolgirl.

INTERVAL

Monsters haunt Dod's dreams. Unspeakable monsters.
Female creatures - but their faces! The features
barely distinguishable as if painted on at the same time
as the make-up, or as if the very function of the make-
up were simply to suggest features, to conceal their
irreparable absence. Deep, rich tints of lunar bright-
ness, the torrid gleam of non-existent lips, long,
endless lashes, excessive yet cunning application of
the darkest eyeliner, immaterial lids heavy with blues
and purples. Yet such animation! Such grace!
Miraculous eyes in which all the nights of summer are
consumed. Oh flame of belladonna...Is it the magnetic
fields set up by their slightest movement? Their gay
and monstrous company gathers about him, scatters
as if at a puff of wind - and next minute they are drifting
dreamily towards him, their flowing robes giving no
hint of their figures, vague, fluctuating beings in whom
Dod fancies he detects a certain indifferent curiosity
regarding him. They approach, brush past him and
are gone, as if immediately distracted by some other
object on which they hasten to bestow the same fleeting
attention. No, they are not hostile. Not yet.

Dod let fall his hand and opened his eyes. Outside the
small uncurtained window a street-lamp, not visible
from his bed, seemed to be spreading not just its
yellowish light but also wreaths of fog out over the
street. A cluster of ghosts uncoiled in a mirror. The
indeterminate room was continually changing its shape,
unable to settle down. Dod had the feeling his bed had
moved while he was asleep and he tried vainly to get
his bearings. For a second he thought he could see
an extension off to the right which could only belong to
some room he did not know or had forgotten. It
disappeared into the shadows...But he had had time
to catch a glimpse of a curious seat which appeared to
be fitted with wheels. Sleep, in the one night, opens
up all rooms, and he says to himself it is a miraculous
enough thing, heaven knows, to wake up in exactly the
place where you fell asleep. And if once there were a
mistake how would one ever know? One always invents
a past for every present.

Abruptly his surroundings abandoned their sinister
dispute and the room became once more familiar, with
its asymmetrical walls and numerous recesses that
gave it the awkward grace of a child's drawing. Dod
wondered to what drunken architect he owed this
charming room and thanked him from the bottom of his
heart. He further remarked to himself that it would
present a geometrical problem of unusual complexity
to anyone who conceived the preposterous idea of trying
to calculate its surface area, and immediately he

pictured the measurers at work: two men in blue with the faces of children.

Kneeling on the floor they would unwind their metal tape-measure, hastily scribble figures in their note-books, add them together, multiply them, puzzle over the results, begin all over again, remeasure everything start arguing in whispers, hurl accusations at one another, and finally turn towards him, their faces dark with suspicion and reproach.

Dod does not understand exactly what the men want.
Who sent them? He looks uncertainly from one to the
other. They could hardly be said to resemble one
another and yet the longer he looks at them the harder
he finds it to distinguish them. He has the impression
of being at the mercy of some optical illusion such as
those produced by certain compositions in which parallel
lines appear to the eye to diverge, or a black square
looks smaller than a white square of the same size.
Although actually this is rather the opposite effect. He
doesn't like it; games like this always end by giving him
a migraine attack. To ward off this threat Dod abandons
the overall view in favour of a detailed examination.
They are both dressed in identical blue boiler-suits
the material of which is so stiff and the colour so deep
that they must be wearing them for the first time.
These garments possess an incredible number of
pockets, all neatly buttoned.
     They did try very hard to explain the purpose of
their visit but in an extremely confused and mumbling
way and on top of that they both started talking at the
same time, which didn't help matters. Now they seem
to be waiting for some answer or sign from him. They
are smiling at him. Perhaps these men are plumbers
come to check the pipes or the water-heater. Dod
indicates the door to the bathroom just in case. They
both turn their heads, exchange looks, and retire to a
corner of the room for a long, whispered confabulation.
They dart a furtive glance at him from time to time,

discover he is watching them, and swiftly look away. Dod, partly out of tact, partly in the hope of putting a stop to their tricks, pretends to lose all interest in their presence. This appears to have the desired effect. The two men separate and start unbuttoning their numerous pockets - not without some difficulty on account of the stiffness of the cloth - taking things out and putting them on the floor at their feet. This goes on for several minutes. Dod is able to identify some of the things: a stop-watch, an electric torch, a railway time-table, a compass, a slide-rule, a tin-opener, a mouth-organ, several ball-point pens, pieces of chalk, some twine... These men are certainly not plumbers, Dod says to himself. But hardly have they got their stuff unpacked than they start putting it away again in their pockets, and with such clumsy haste that things slip out of their hands; balls of twine come undone, sheets of paper go flying, other objects roll across the floor. Dod doesn't know whether to be amused or frightened by this appalling lack of co-ordination. Now one of the men has trodden on his stop-watch. He picks it up and shows the other man the damage. They both utter gloomy cries.

A certain amount of progress, however, seems to have been made and something very like a job is well under way. The two men are now on their knees. One takes the end of a metal tape-measure and the other unwinds it until it reaches the wall. There he bends down to read off the figures and Dod is surprised all of a sudden to hear him distinctly enunciate: 'Four hundred and forty.'

The two men look up simultaneously and exchange incredulous glances. Then they turn towards Dod as if expecting him to furnish an explanation. Dod feels vaguely guilty, but without knowing what of he is at a loss to exculpate himself. He is on the point of suggesting that perhaps it is not as bad as they think and that one should beware of drawing hasty conclusions

46

from a first measurement; if the gentlemen cared to begin again they would certainly arrive at a more suitable figure which they could then - he appreciates their scruples - add to the first and thus, by dividing the resultant sum by two, obtain an average. And an average is frequently a means of avoiding the worst.

However, the one who was holding the end of the tape has laid a large dictionary on it to keep it in place and has crawled on his knees to join his companion. Together, heads touching, they check the result, and then launch into a fresh confabulation. Finally they get to their feet and Dod now has a distinct impression that they are avoiding his eye. This worries him. One of the men writes down the result of the measurement in a note-book; the other takes a compass out of his pocket and indicates a direction with his arm. They both get down on their knees again and unwind the tape-measure.

Suddenly the men begin to display enormous agility. Attached by their metal tape-measure they move about the room tracing figures from some complex ballet, kneeling down and getting up again with such fluidity of movement as to suggest they have overcome the forces of gravity, looking about them and then, with an expression of immemorial experience and deep sagacity on their faces, gliding off to other points of the room to take fresh measurements, the results of which are immediately noted down.

Dod is puzzled. He can understand neither the method they are working on nor why they take a measurement in one direction rather than in another. The actual shape and dimensions of his room appear to interest them so little that he begins to wonder whether they are not following the capricious outline of some imaginary room. Twice Dod's chair is in their way; they move it just enough to allow them passage, taking great care and stammering excuses. Coming across it a third time, however, without further ado they

47

shove it right into a corner and Dod finds he is left
facing the wall. He dare not protest. He can, by
craning his neck round as far as it will go to right or
left, get a partial view of operations, but the gymnastics
involved are so painful that he soon gives up. He
guesses that the two men are now at either end of the
room's principal axis, one by the door and the other by
the window. Suddenly, in tones of infinite amazement,
separating each syllable, the latter announces: 'Seven
hundred and seventy-two.' The other answers with a
strangled cry. Dod hears a confused scrambling noise
and catches a few fleeting words which he takes to
mean that the measurers have come to the wrong
address.

Then he hears the door slam.

Dod is alone in the now silent room. He could
excuse the men's carelessness for the distraction they
brought him, but he is not at all happy about the way
they have left him in a corner, like a child in disgrace,
with nothing to occupy his thoughts or divert him
except this lithograph on the wall, which he has gazed
at so often in other circumstances when he didn't feel
under any obligation to do so, depicting a narrow
winding street in the old town with crooked paving-stones
and lop-sided houses, a single lamp-post standing out
as a dark line against the shaded background, its
antiquated form dating back to the era of gas-lighting.
No details can be seen that might substantiate this
impression but a subtle inflexion in the treatment of
space suggests that the sea is not far away, which is
enough to indicate that this street is situated in the
harbour district.

Dod fixes his attention on the solitary figure which
can be made out towards the far end of the street, a
figure whose diminutive stature he had thought up to
now to have been no more than a normal effect of the
play of perspective; but looking at it closely, something he has never done before, he realizes that this

character really is small, and just as his gaze is
beginning to waver with fatigue he is able to distinguish,
through a jumble of subtly suggestive lines, the mis-
shapen silhouette of a hunch-backed dwarf.

Dod, standing by the window, watched the dwarf moving
off. Once past the uncertain limit of the dense yellow
light cast by the street-lamp, he appeared to dissolve
in the fog.

Dod hesitated no more than a second before rushing
to the door, just allowing himself time to wonder why
the little monster had given him such a feeling of déjà
vu - the fact that one tends to confuse all individuals
of a similar type and remember them only for what
they have in common was too natural an explanation to
satisfy him - and also to wonder what it had been doing
on the pavement opposite, looking up at his window
without moving, as if it has been posted there for
some mysterious surveillance.

Reaching the street, Dod strained his ears in vain
for the slightest sound of footsteps. The dwarf had
gone off in the direction of the harbour but his dumpy
legs could not have got him far. Dod shivered. He
reflected that it would be better to go back and fetch
an overcoat or, to be entirely reasonable, go to bed.
But having spent the early hours of the evening asleep,
which he did not usually do, and since he felt wonderfully eager and alert, and above all because it is enough
to start moving for an impulse to become a body in
motion, off he went at a run.

He was brought up short at the intersection of the
Rue Athanase and the Rue du Bain, in two minds as to
which way to take. Straight ahead the Rue du Bain
changed its name and became the Rue de la Soufflerie,
a narrow alley which disappeared in the direction of
the wharves. Fog and deep shadows sealed it off.
The Rue Athanase, wider and better lit, was deserted
as far as the eye could see to right and left. Reflecting

once more that he would do better to go home to bed, Dod turned to the left.

He had gone barely a hundred yards before he caught sight of the dwarf's silhouette ahead of him. He adjusted his pace to keep the figure just within view but even so found he had to keep moving fairly fast; the creature had an astonishing turn of speed for one so small. A little farther on Dod lost sight of him and broke into a run again.

The dwarf had turned down the Rue de la Tête-Noire and Dod reached the cross-roads just in time to see him change direction again, taking the Rue du Capitaine-Mather. This street ran down to the Quai des Cygnes which was lined with restaurants, bars, night-clubs and sailors' haunts, most of them open all night. Neon signs stained the fog with blood. The dwarf disappeared from view in a crowd of revellers who had just come out of one of these establishments, and when Dod reached the spot he found himself outside the Lovely Lady Tavern. A few steps led down to a door below street-level.

'My son has never been anything but a comfort to me, I must say. Motherhood has filled my cup with blessings.'

She gives the words time to release this feeling of plenitude within her, saturates herself with it, and then freezes - and her skin appears suddenly as if covered with a film of varnish. This is eternity.

Up in the cathedral's stained-glass windows, doves and angels bear away a woman who is beyond amazement.

A little air let out in a long sigh recalls the uncertain concatenations of life. The vertigo of interrupted assumptions...But she, with an instinct sharpened by experience, avoids the fall and alights gently on a half-landing.

Smiling, she says, 'His teachers thought very highly of him.'

Examining this sentence for what she can draw from it, she finds this: 'Le Bocage School has always had excellent teachers. They had to have proved themselves for several years before they were sent to our little town, and then they frequently stayed on until their retirement. Great care was taken to keep up the school's old reputation and many pupils came from far away to pursue their secondary education there. It was a tradition in all the best families.'

'I'm going to go to high school too,' says the schoolgirl, 'to learn massage and kinetic therapy, and maybe midwifery.'

'Like Mme Arthème?'

'Is Mme Arthème a midwife?'

'Mme Arthème was midwife in our little town. It was she who helped me bring my son into the world. She used to say she had never seen such a beautiful baby.'

The schoolgirl steals a glance at Dod and says anxiously, 'You must have suffered a lot.'

'Yes, a great deal,' says his mother, 'but I have been greatly recompensed.'

'Sometimes,' says the schoolgirl, 'babies come out feet first.'

'Well, bless me if the little girl doesn't know all about it,' exclaims his mother, turning to Dod.

'I'm not going to have any children,' decides the schoolgirl. 'It's too dangerous. I'm going to look after other people's children. When Mme Arthème dies I'll go on looking after your son.'

His mother is very taken with this.

'Do you hear?' she says to Dod. 'Aren't you the lucky man!'

Dod smiles and shows by his expression that he is pleased. He tells himself the schoolgirl may easily die before Mme Arthème. But noticing that the little girl has her eyes on him he blushes, feeling disturbed and uneasy.

'Can your son have children?'

'What a question,' says his mother. 'He's still too young to start thinking in those terms. We'll see about that when he's completed his studies.'

And her look conveys to the schoolgirl that it would be indiscreet to pursue the matter further.

Silence has fallen in the darkening room. His mother is musing. The schoolgirl is invisible again. Dod turns towards the lights of the buildings opposite. So many lives...he says to himself. But his imagination does not respond to the lead. Other people are too far away. He dimly remembers a time when the world

52

was full of voices, laughter, many presences. Each encounter cut a new facet on life...Or was he dreaming? The world, now, is this desert, these apparitions, and he, their object. Certainly, he says to himself, there was some time or other when I was lost in wonder.

But his mother is talking.

'We were happy in our little town. Each autumn I used to make my own jams and preserves for the whole year. They used to fill a large oak cupboard we had. And people would bring us things from the neighbouring farms - milk, eggs, home-cured bacon...We didn't have any of these chemical products then. But life has changed so much and things will never again be what they were. That was before Dod left us. Oh, the torments with which I looked forward to that separation. It had to be, his father used to say...'

She passes a hand over her face and with a great deal of compassion for herself goes on: 'I don't really know whether I'm coming or going any more. I get everything mixed up. It's true he left us on two occasions. We mothers have only our poor hearts and our daily tasks to fall back on. When Dod passed his baccalauréat, with distinction, of course he had to leave us to continue his studies in the School of Pharmacy at the old university. Later on, when the time came, he was to have taken over from his father. His father was a pharmacist. It's a good profession, though one that carries heavy responsibilities. Once established my Dod would have married some girl from our little town and we would have gone on living happily together... Yet I couldn't overcome my apprehensions and I kept thinking of the child living on his own in that treacherous Babylon, breathing those unhealthy northern fogs, making dubious acquaintances, so many worries for a mother, and him so trusting, so inexperienced... Well, when I saw my Dod again he hadn't changed - still the same modest manner and that transparent expression which showed you everything he was thinking.

It was the sixth of July when he came back, the day
before the Le Bocage festival...'

She pauses, flustered.

'Oh dear,' she says, 'my poor old brain. He'd
already been back several times, Christmas, Easter...
I'm getting everything muddled up.'

She mutters to herself for a moment, counting on
her fingers. Time, for her, is continually contracting
and facts have merged together in her memory to form
a pebble which hardens with every day that passes.
Then her face lights up.

'It was two years later,' she says. 'The Le Bocage
festival was to be a particularly splendid one that year,
it being our high school's centenary. Dod wouldn't
have missed such an occasion for anything in the world,
and many former pupils who today occupy eminent
positions in business, the arts, industry or public
office went out of their way to mark the solemn event
with their presence.'

Her eyes shine as she recalls this brilliant page in
the annals of Le Bocage.

'After speeches from the headmaster, the mayor and
the representative of the Ministry of Education we had
the prize-giving and then a gymnastic display in the
quadrangle...Nothing special,' she added with a smile,
'but it was all so charming, so thrilling. Even the
teachers seemed to be enjoying themselves. And in
the evening we all gathered at the Municipal Theatre...'

Dod says to himself he simply must get hold of that
course in comparative literature. Putting it off day
after day...

'...Not for a long time had our old theatre witnessed
such a celebration. Everything was a-glitter...'

Olivier is sure to call by in the morning. Remember
to ask him...

'...Many of the gentlemen were in evening dress and
the ladies were all wearing their jewellery. Oh, it was
a quite unforgettable scene! People waved to one

another from box to box, made signs to one another...'

Can one still count on him, though? Poor old Olivier... Poor? He's happy. Blessed are the poor in spirit... Or sense... Mum doesn't like him...

'... There was a camel... That would be rather extraordinary, though, wouldn't it? A camel on the stage... I must be muddling things... I can't remember. At any rate the whole thing was very oriental... Yes, now I remember the dwarf. He had an enormous hump on his back and he escorted the queen... How silly of me, it was obviously the dwarf put me in mind of a camel...'

Wouldn't it be better to ask Isabelle? With Olivier in his present state...

'... In the middle of the performance Dod was taken ill...'

Isabelle or Jamyne... Must be five or six days since he saw Jamyne, though... Dod becomes aware of a change in the quality of space and tells himself he is about to have another migraine attack.

'... Dr. Nauser is himself a former pupil of Le Bocage... We knew his father extremely well. Dod couldn't have fallen into better hands. It is said that his clients include cabinet ministers, writers... We were very lucky indeed that he decided to take an interest in our son. Next day... I believe it was the next day... He took him away in his car... and he told us not to worry about the financial side, saying he would look after that himself... in remembrance of the deep friendship between us and his father... and because he was keen to keep under observation such a curious case of... Oh dear, these scientific terms... Yes, I believe it was the next day Dr. Nauser took him off to his clinic. The annoying thing was that Dod had to interrupt his studies. But at his age...'

She shrugs.

'Mme Arthème has been Dr. Nauser's assistant for several years now...'

She mumbles a few further words and then dozes off.
The schoolgirl is invisible once more. Dod turns
towards the window and watches the migraine flares
dancing in the fog.

As Dod entered the Lovely Lady the fog swirled in with him. At least that was his impression, for so smoky was the atmosphere and so loud the confused roar of voices that he was brought to an abrupt halt on the threshold as if he had encountered a solid obstacle, his eyes meanwhile groping towards the far end of the room, peering down its whole length in a vain attempt to get the measure of its indistinct limits. The space between was packed to an incredible density, alive with ponderous gestures and swiftly moving shadows.

Dod plunged into the throng. As he moved everything moved, all shapes and distances existing in a constant state of flux - then he saw why, noticing that every step drew him into the self-perpetuating ambush of the huge mirrors that lined the walls. It was not long either before he noticed that the tavern did not consist of this room only but continued in another larger and if possible even noisier room going off to the left. On a dais at the corner three musicians - a pianist, a saxaphonist and a drummer - could just be heard above the din playing antiquated dance music.

Dod moved over to the bar. The cashier, a huge and beautiful woman, flashed him a smile. He noticed a picture on the wall behind her, its colours dulled by a layer of filth: flowers in a blue vase - datura, he thought they were.

Dod, perched on a tall stool, began cautiously to size up his surroundings. Faces were raised from time to time into the amber light but he was unable to

fix on them long enough to make out their features.
The lighting was such as to favour the most subtle
play of shadow, and so swiftly did it snatch people and
things from his view that he was left with the impression
that it moved with his gaze. The occasional abruptly
raised voice would isolate a gesticulating figure and
next moment a fresh wave of sound would break heavily
over it and bury him in the solid mass of the rest of
the group. Waiters in white jackets were gliding about
between the tables.

Possibly because it was larger, or for quite another
reason, the second room appeared to be even darker,
and Dod wondered who were the indiscernible occupants
of the cubicles at the back where red-shaded lamps
threw glowing shadows.

'Your first visit to the Lovely Lady?'

At a table near the bar, three solemn-looking grey-
haired gentlemen were sitting around an ice-bucket
from which protruded an unopened bottle of champagne,
the object of their mistrustful gaze. They held themselves stiffly upright in their chairs, and although
there was no real resemblance between them their
similarity of bearing, posture and expression lent them
a strange conformity. One of these gentlemen Dod
thought he recognized as his old mathematics master
from Le Bocage School, an impression that was
strengthened by the furtive and irritated glances which
the man threw at him from time to time.

Dod was wondering whether he should acknowledge
this recognition by some discreetly deferential sign,
even if it were only a nod, or whether on the other
hand courtesy demanded that he refrain from doing so,
when the waiter arrived and set about uncorking the
bottle.

Glasses in hand, the three gentlemen lost a little of
their stiffness. One by one, wreathed in benign smiles,
they took turns to hold forth.

Dod has just switched on his television. It is a
portable model, made in China, covered in brown
leather and fitted with a remote control. It was
delivered yesterday. The cardboard box is still
standing in the corner and Dod makes a mental note to
keep it for some of the books which will not fit into
his book-case or on the shelves.

The picture wobbles for a moment and then holds.
The screen is occupied by a man leaning with his elbows
on a desk, finger-tips just touching. Dod experiences
a faint tremor of excitement at watching his first tele-
vised lecture. Perhaps soon, thanks to the initiative
of some cameraman too young to leave his apparatus
still for long, he will be given a view of the lecture-
room itself with a chance of recognizing here and there
a face he knows - Isabelle's, maybe, or Olivier's,
why not?

The man is talking. That is to say his lips are
moving: Dod has forgotten to turn up the sound. But
he is in no hurry to remedy his error and start working
and taking notes; he decides to allow himself a moment's
light relief. He is fascinated by this man talking. He
watches the thin lips shaping the inaudible words, the
eyebrows lifting for a pause - the eyes becoming empty
then and the man's immobility taking on the quality of
a photograph - then, the lecturer having at last found
the right expression, leaning forward and swallowing
up the audience with his gaze, the lips resuming their
movement, hurrying on, the hands suddenly flying apart,

the right hand describing a peremptory accompaniment
to several seconds of earnest affirmation.

Delighted, Dod prolongs the game. Sometimes at
Le Bocage School he used to shut his mind to what the
master was saying, separating him from the substance
of his lecture, from his function, and even from his
identity, achieving in the end a kind of deliciously
incongruous vocal and gesticulatory phenomenon which
he would then observe with detachment.

He is just promising himself that he will explore the
possibilities of television further in this direction when
he is bothered by a vague feeling that something is
wrong. He bows to the facts: the face he is looking at
is not that of Professor Massoret. This man on the
screen is someone he has never seen before in his life.

Dod turns up the sound and finds himself in the middle
of a lecture on common law. He looks at his watch,
wonders for a moment if it really is Wednesday today,
and is forced to conclude that they have changed the
programme. He is at a loss. His time-table is
completely thrown out. So confused is he in fact that
he goes on listening uncomprehendingly to the man
who is now talking about the disposable portion of the
estate and the last survivor, about liberalities and
acceptance under beneficium inventorii, ultra vires
hereditatis, and then suddenly the words hit him, and
it is so utterly unexpected he tells himself in vain it's
nerves, it's ridiculous, he cannot anyhow control the
trembling fit that has taken hold of him, the sick feeling,
the dizziness, and it's no good saying to himself it's a
migraine attack, his knuckles are white on the arms
of his chair as the terrifying voice repeats over and
over again: the dead man distrains upon the living.
He has, however, by reflex action, turned off the set.
Then he hears the door opening.

Tiny footsteps can be heard moving across the room.
Dod slumps in his chair.

'Ah, it's come at last,' exclaims his mother. 'The

60

screen does look rather small, though. That's the
trouble with these portable sets, and even so they cost
more than the others though one wonders why. You've
got a remote control, of course, that's essential.'

She sits down, adding: 'Well, anyway, I hope it will
give you pleasure.'

Then she takes an envelope from her handbag,
searches for her glasses and eventually finds them.

'I have here a letter from your aunt Lea. She is
deeply concerned about you, as you'll see. Listen:

'"My dearest Lili,

'"I have received your letter and am very happy to
have such good news of you all. I cannot, however,
help feeling a certain anxiety. Despite what you tell
me about Dod and about the very marked improvement
in his health I have the impression that the child
continues to give you great cause for concern. Reading
your letter I was aware of a certain reluctance on your
part to talk to me about him, and the vagueness with
which you expressed yourself could hardly fail to
arouse my suspicions."'

'Your aunt is an extremely shrewd person,' says
his mother and resumes her reading:

'"But you know my feelings on the subject. You
have always been too weak with him and his illness
has not improved matters. I fail to understand how you
could both bring yourselves to let him leave in that
state. Because really that business about his studies
was just so much nonsense. I admit there is no longer
any question of his taking over the pharmacy - although
in this as in everything else one should avoid jumping
to premature conclusions - but you must surely agree
that the idea of reading for a degree in literature is
the purest fantasy. What it comes down to is that he
does exactly what he wants and you say amen to it.
David is not exactly a fool but I sometimes ask myself
whether he takes his role as a father seriously. The
way that man thinks is beyond me."'

His mother smiles indulgently. 'Your aunt has never been very fond of your father,' she says.

"'However I miss you both very much and await your return with impatience. I only hope that Dod has the sense to come back with you and so put a stop to an episode which it is my opnion has already gone on far too long.

"'But now I have some very surprising news for you. It is probable, not to say certain, that you will be seeing the little Moran sisters before you return. No doubt you find this impossible to imagine and I swear to you it was the very last thing I expected. But these dear sweet creatures, for whom a walk to the cemetery was a major expedition, have suddenly decided to tuck up their skirts and go dashing off to explore the big city. When they told me of their plans I wondered at first whether I shouldn't burst out laughing, but they were quite serious, and I said to myself why not indeed, it would do them no harm at all to get out and enjoy themselves a bit, having only ever lived for other people before. And I am by no means sorry that they have decided to sow their wild oats under your wing so to speak because the poor dears are so inexperienced. I believe they will be writing to you soon, that is to say that Louise will write while Clotilde dictates, as usual, on account of the glasses."

'I do indeed find it hard to believe,' says his mother. 'Your aunt is quite right about it being a surprising piece of news.' She is thoughtful for a moment. 'It's a long time since you last saw your cousins.'

Various images float to the surface of Dod's mind, fleeting images which immediately dissolve into confused impressions. One memory, however, takes shape, and suddenly he recognizes the stiff and uncomfortable feeling he used to experience when wearing his best suit, with a tie knotted too tightly round his neck. It must have been a Sunday. The maid had just shown them into a dimly lit room where the shutters

were all closed, and it seemed to him all the more
dark and cool because he had been walking for a long
time in the sun. The room smelled musty but with a
certain indefinable nuance rather like the odour of
antiseptic. His parents stood motionless beside him
and he could hear his father's laboured breathing. A
piping of high voices made him look up. At the end of
the room there was a staircase and half-way up it he
saw two creatures with tiny faces leaning over the
wooden banister. Their black hair was drawn up on
top of their heads in a solid bun that bristled with pins
and combs, and they were both laughing and talking at
the same time.

But then another image, older probably and less
distinct, disturbs this vision. Standing beside his
cousins or possibly a little way behind them is another
woman, also dressed in black, and although he cannot
make out her features he feels very strongly that she
is much younger than her two sisters.

'What about Amélie?' he asks abruptly.

His mother gives a start. She looks at him earnestly
for a moment. Then she murmurs, 'You remember
Amélie?'

Dod indicates by a wave of the hand how vague his
memory of Amélie has by now become.

'Amélie,' says his mother slowly, 'Amélie is dead.'

Dod gives a nod and insists no further. He knows
that sometimes one speaks of the dead but that no one
ever speaks of Amélie.

'But I haven't finished reading the letter,' says his
mother.

Before she can begin reading again Dod asks, 'What
does she mean - "on account of the glasses"?'

'On account of the glasses?' repeats his mother.

'Aunt Lea says they will be writing to you and that...'

'On account of the glasses! Yes, I know...' His
mother laughs softly. 'Oh dear, the poor things, like
everyone else they have their little eccentricities.

You see they've only ever had one pair of glasses
between them which they take it in turns to wear
according to who needs them. Writing letters is the
prerogative of Clotilde, she being the elder sister -
each of them, you know, has her own very clearly
defined responsibilities; their whole life is a model
of organization - but on the other hand the glasses in
question are not so well adapted to her sight as they
are to Louise's, so that they tire her eyes if she wears
them for any length of time. Consequently it is Louise
who writes the letters while Clotilde dictates. It's a
little foible that has always very much amused your
aunt and myself.'

She gives another little chuckle and then goes on
reading:

"'Léone comes to see me twice a week. She brings
me vegetables from the garden and each time she comes
she never fails to ask whether I have had a letter from
you. Poor Léone is getting very aged. She used to
keep me in touch with gossip in our little town, and
heaven knows I have little enough to distract me, but
for some time now this has consisted of no more than
telling me that M. or Mme So-and-so has just passed
away, and that makes her feel sorry for herself and
she starts telling me about her own troubles which as
you can guess grow daily more numerous. She would
so much like to see Dod back. To tell you the truth
there have been a great many deaths here this autumn.
The early cold spells have left many gaps and I am
beginning to feel quite lonely. So, my dearest Lili,
you must not stay away too long. My fondest greetings
to you all. "'

His mother folds the letter, replaces it in its
envelope, puts the envelope back in her bag and says:
'You see.'

DOCUMENT

Belladonna, fair flower, star of the Sabbath, our
strength and wisdom, for today at least, greetings.
In your pentasegmental gamopetalous corolla gleams
the royal purple of our dreams - but this is beyond
the perception of the uninitiated. The pale-eyed
botanist will be content to note your dull red colouring
or the reniform seeds of your fruit, and perhaps his
old heart will palpitate to see your villous leaves on
their short petioles, oval, alternating, occasionally
geminate. He will describe you with all the exactitude
of the serious man of letters, and with no ulterior
motive. He will certainly not overlook the fact that
the poison is concentrated principally in your fleshy
root - oh blessed poison that permeates you through-
out, leaves, fruit, even flowers secreting the delicious
sap - but it would never occur to him to nibble that
root with his yellow, tobacco-stained teeth to see if it
is by any chance true what they say. And what do they
say? They say that in the event of belladonna poisoning
it is advisable, while waiting for the doctor, to provoke
vomiting by irritation of the uvula.
     The doctor arrives and it is Dr. Nauser. He
immediately carries the patient off in his black Mercedes,
and when he has gone the members of his family take
out the photographs of the departed and begin to look
at them. At the clinic he is handed over to Mme
Arthème - she knows what to do. One by one she will
eradicate the dreams which the belladonna has fostered.
Using long needles she will inject into him at set times

the antidotes which will be borne by his blood into the most intimate corners of his brain. In a few days the patient begins to urinate normally again.

Mme Arthème's task is not yet complete. She knows that some of the poison always remains, that the most thorough course of treatment can never remove all trace of it, and that in every case, no matter how pains takingly the dreamer has been cleansed of his dreams, one or two tiny eggs survive, wanting no more than the chance to hatch out. And that is why she ceaselessly patrols the town with her syringes and her long needles the vigilant guardian of men's sleep.

What reveller, stupid with drink and the laughter of women, has not encountered her at least once in the grey dawn streets and, seeing that face of marble, felt his heart sink at the sudden reminder of his childhood? Hers is no easy job.

Alkaloids, belladonna's ardent spirits, wings of the witch, I leave to others the task of itemizing your virtues. Ah but atropine, white flame dedicated to the youngest, she who cuts the thread between the sleeper and his dream, and it's the sleeper flies away!

Before leaving for the Sabbath the witches used to anoin their bodies with an unguent of belladonna. Then a breath of wind would carry them away. They flew howling over the countryside pursued by the barking of dogs starting up out of sleep, above sleeping towns fringed with graveyards, and sometimes, down in a deserted street, they caught sight of Mme Arthème's grey cape. She who is also known as Balthasar, rouse abruptly from her meditations, looks up and observes that something is going on. Indeed before long she can discern, floating at an altitude calculated to defy both the laws of physics and the precepts of morality, a knot of naked bodies with bums of excessive protuberar and breasts turgescent with pleasure. She has seen

many things in her life, she who is ageless, but this
robs her of her composure notwithstanding. She hurls
a fist at the sky, her lips writhing in silent imprecation.
The witches, inspired by this outburst of impotent rage,
their bodies all the madder for being unrestrained by
weight, throw themselves into a variety of lubricious
postures before the irresistible breath of the belladonna
carries them off and away to the nuptials of the king
and queen.

Your light, oh belladonna, shone in the eyes of the
loveliest women of Rome, whose lovers were not long
in dying for reasons unknown.

(Fragment of a study for a lyrical pharmacopoeia
found among Dod's papers after his last disappearance
and probably dating back to the period when the young
man was thinking of becoming a pharmacist like his
father.)

'Your first visit to the Lovely Lady?'

A hand had been placed on his. Dod turned and smiled pleasantly. He was smiling too at his own confusion and at the faint anguish he had experienced at being asked whether this was his first visit to the Lovely Lady. He told himself the formula was probably this enterprising young person's habitual opening gambit. She appeared to be in no hurry to press her advantage, however, continuing to observe him with a curious insistence. Too sure of herself, possibly, and of her power. Summoning, in order to conceal his embarrassment, all the detachment he was capable of affecting, Dod decided to reciprocate the attention to which he was being subjected. But he fell into the trap - those eyes. And it was as if he had plunged into the final night of the end of time and in his heart was no other desire than to be lost irrevocabl' drawn ever farther by that gaze which seemed to come out of some prodigious distance like the flickering light of a star that has been dead for millions of years. Nothing existed at that moment but those eyes, their pupils so dilated as almost to have swallowed up the iris.

Suddenly, the way a man leaning out over emptiness, gripping the edge of the parapet with his hands, hurls his body backwards to shake off the dizziness, Dod said: 'Will you have something to drink?'

It had the desired effect and she looked away. Dod took a deep breath. A vague feeling of resentment

sharpened his glance as he permitted himself an
inspection as rapid as it was pitiless, noting the slightly
crumpled pale pink dress, the professional décolleté,
the magnificent shining blonde hair, probably dyed,
the tired look about her features which the make-up,
excessive though it was, could not conceal. The
woman was clearly much older than he had at first
supposed. But this he immediately regretted. Although
he knew that she was paid to do so he felt flattered by
the interest she took in him. He wanted to find her
beautiful and searched for ways to excuse her for not
being as beautiful as he could have wished. Obviously,
he told himself, with the life she leads.... He pictured
it to himself: the men, the drinking... Then it occurred
to him to wonder whether such a life really was so
tiring. He had once heard Kell say that a hostess drinks
much less than the common man - the common man,
that day, being Dod - might suppose, and that, as far
as alcohol was concerned, most of the time such women
drank a mixture prepared especially for their benefit
containing no alcohol at all. Up to a point Kell's
experience could be relied upon.

The barman must have been on the look-out. She
beckoned and he came over.

'Two whiskies please, Dino.'

Dod was on the point of asking for a beer, not because
he particularly wanted one but simply as a childish
assertion of independence. In the end he merely sighed
at the thought of what he would have to pay for the drinks.
The woman was looking at him again.

'Are you a student?' But it was more a statement
than a question.

'Is it so obvious?'

'A lot of students come here.' And in the expressionless tone with which one conveys information which is
useful but not indispensable she added, 'I'm Amalia.'

He wondered whether he should give his name too
and in his hesitation adopted a vacant expression and

looked away. In doing so he met the indignant glare
of his old maths master or, if it was not he, a man
who appeared to be endowed with a similarly irritable
nature. Just at that moment the woman replaced
her hand on his. He felt himself blush. And then, for
the first time, she smiled.

'I think I've seen you before,' she said. And very
quickly, as if interrupting herself, she added, 'What's
your subject?'

'Pharmacy,' he said.

'Are you going to be a pharmacist?'

She had leant across towards him and he could smell
her perfume. It was an intricate blend of subtly
dissonant odours in which he caught a trace of musk
and also, for a moment, a brief effluvium which he was
unable to identify but which he associated with dark,
secluded places, with solitude and silence; it was like
the smell of freshly turned earth. It suddenly struck
him that he had smelled something like it once when
he was a child, and he recalled the strange and melancholy thoughts that had disturbed him on that rainy
Sunday in July, the eve of his departure for Hampshire,
probably, because he had been taken to visit his cousins
in their large, ramshackle house on the outskirts of
town. He had been given a weak cup of tea and some
mildewed cakes. He was bored. After an hour of
sitting still and being good he had got up. Waiting
another minute or two to make sure no one was paying
any attention to him, he had left his parents with the
old spinsters and gone exploring. He already knew
all the ground-floor rooms, none of which held any
mystery for him, so he had immediately proceeded
upstairs. There he had looked into two rooms in
succession cluttered with furniture and bric-a-brac
and a smell of mouldiness and decay had made him
screw up his nose; it was the same smell as bothered
him every time he was kissed by his cousins. Then,
opening a third door, he had found himself in a room

where the shutters were closed. It was almost empty; the only piece of furniture was a bare bed. And a strange, numb feeling had come over him. Standing there motionless and bewildered in that cold, dark, cave-like room which seemed besieged on all sides by the drumming rain, he had drifted imperceptibly through space and time to that day when he had opened the shutters and seen Mrs. Mabel Crocker-Jones standing beneath her large red umbrella by the white fence around the house in Hampshire.

All of a sudden, without really realizing what he was doing, he had gone over to the window and tried to push open the shutters. But he had come up against the resistance of a dense mass of foliage and could open them only a little way. A strong smell of damp earth filled the room. Overcome by dizziness he had closed his eyes.

He had turned round to find Clotilde standing in the doorway. She was staring at him with a queer expression of hatred a fear. Then with a twisted smile she had said, 'Little boy, you're too inquisitive.'

She had come swiftly across the room towards him and an icy hand had seized his wrist.

As they were going downstairs she had blithely explained to him that that was the only room facing due north and that it was therefore particularly damp and cold, even at the height of summer; he could have caught his death of cold there. She had gone on to say that if he was naughty again she would lock him in the cellar.

A LETTER FROM OLIVIER

Dod old friend,
Just a couple of words. Everything's happening so
fast. I've been home with her and been introduced to
her parents...What an ordeal! Luckily Alwyn was
there. Heavens, though...It's all happening too fast.
How much longer can we go on living with such immedia
in the present - the wonderful present? I can already
feel all the insidious threads dragging us down to
everydayness. But we'll be together again in an hour
or so, and again tomorrow, and she's spending the
night or New Year's Eve at Bob's place. What more
could I want?

I haven't forgotten about you, though. I've had a
word with Alwyn. Old man, it's impossible, you can't
have known Mabel Crocker-Jones - she died practically
half a century ago. A remarkable woman, as far as I
can make out, who made a big name for herself on
the stage in her day, and an even bigger name off it.
The family are rather reluctant to talk about her. Who
else could have told you about her except Redstone?
Apparently the old fool speaks of her as if he could
still see her - dixit Alwyn.

Bye for now,

Olivier

P.S. I didn't intend telling you this here but anyway...
Mabel Crocker-Jones' stage-name was Mary Seymour.
But you're a sane enough chap not to dwell on the
coincidence, I'm sure.

'Look who I've brought to see you, son. How's that for a surprise, eh? How's that for a splendid surprise? Eh?' His father is absolutely chortling with glee.

Dod feels the chair slam against his back as if he had been subjected to an acceleration of several G. In three strides Dr. Nauser is in the centre of the room. He looks around him, beaming.

'But this isn't bad at all. No sir, this is not bad at all. Living like a lord.'

He goes over to the window, draws back the curtains.

'And what a view! Congratulations!'

His father is now dancing with glee.

'South-western aspect. Well, what do you think of it? I can't tell you how pleased I am...' He leans towards Dod. 'Just coming out of the station and who should I bump into... But you haven't seen the kitchen and bathroom.'

Was it the walk in the cold or is it excitement? He is extremely red in the face. Already he is throwing open doors. Dr. Nauser drops into a chair and stretches his long legs voluptuously. One of his feet knocks against the wheel of Dod's chair.

'Well, my young friend, you're looking superbly fit. David, you didn't tell me how superbly fit your son was looking. He's enjoying himself, the rogue.'

His father wipes his eyes, sighs, and says with a smile, 'I'm delighted you find him in such good shape, Alexandre.'

Dr. Nauser bends forward and jabs a fleshy hand at

Dod's legs.

'Amazing.'

He leans back again and the chair creaks dangerously
Dod's father is watching him anxiously.

'Not a trace of muscular atrophy. And how long is it
now since he last used his tiny legs? David, this young
dog's been holding out on us. He gets up every night
for a spot of gymnastics.'

His father laughs, weeps, and again wipes his eyes.

'What a doctor you are! What a doctor!' He turns
towards Dod. 'Your mother has had another letter
from Clotilde. They've put off their departure yet
again. On account of the cold or some reason. I
doubt whether they'll ever make up their minds. This
is the little Moran sisters, Alexandre - you must
remember them.'

Dr. Nauser gives a nod. His expression is one of
quite unusual benevolence. He nods again and smiles.

'Yes indeed, indeed. Clotilde, Louise and...'
Dod's father starts making desperate signals. 'Do you
know I sometimes miss our little town? One day I'm
going to drop all this, all this empty bustle...They've
got the right idea, the Moran sisters, never stirring
from their little nest.'

He stands up and unbuttons his expensive overcoat.
Dod's father rushes to help him off with it and then
lays it carefully on the bed.

'Just look at this young rascal, David. He got
the message too that the best thing...He's thumbing
his nose at us and my God he's right. Eh, you blighter,
aren't you thumbing your nose at us? You're living
like a fighting cock and you wouldn't have it any
different for all the treasures of the Queen of Sheba.'

Dr. Nauser's mighty laugh fills the room. Dod's
father laughs too - a little. Then he asks anxiously,
'Alexandre, you don't think he'll be spending the rest
of his life...'

'I don't think anything, my friend. What are you

74

worried about, anyway? He's happy, isn't he? In
any case you've sold your business now, which between
you and me proves a number of things.' He leans
towards Dod. 'You're a cultured lad...Didn't your
father tell me you were reading for a degree in literature -
and why not, for heaven's sake? You've obviously
profited by Blaise Pascal's reflection: All the unhappiness
of man...And what is the good Mme Arthème up to?'

'Well,' says his father, 'we have every reason to be
satisfied...'

'I've rather lost touch with her...like so many others.'
Dr. Nauser strokes his large nose with one finger.

'I've been travelling around a bit this last year giving
lectures - been enjoying myself, too. I've just spent
three months in London where I have many friends.
That reminds me...' He turns to Dod, 'It was in
London that I ran into one of your pals - you'll forgive
me for having forgotten his name, especially since he
for his part pretended not to recognize me. The
scoundrel was having a beer in a pub and getting all
worked up over an old hen. No, actually a young hen.
But the fact remains that as far as women are concerned
I know few boys of your age who have any taste at all.
You, my young friend, are of course one of them, in
spite of...David - ever thought of finding him an
attachment...some nice girl who likes a steady life?
I mean, hell, he's got his glands...'

'Really Alexandre...if his mother could hear you!'

'Ah, the admirable Lili! Did I ask you how she was?
Yes, I believe I did. In any case I have no worries on
that score - she's cut out to be a widow.'

This time Dod's father is visibly shocked.

'Oh, I beg your pardon, dear old friend, I didn't
know you still attached any importance to all that. Did
I tell you I'm planning to go back into practice in the
old town? Of course...' He breaks off and smiles at
an idea which he finds amusing. '...I shall confine
myself to investigating a handful of interesting cases.

In confidence David' - he gives Dod's father a wink -
'I've started to write a book summing up my modest
experience and I need to complete certain observations
which I've been able to make.' He taps the wheel of
Dod's chair with his foot. 'That, my young friend,
will give me an excuse for taking you in hand once
more.'

His father says, 'I never really understood, Alexand
why in fact you closed your clinic.'

'I got married for a while. You see, I've always
hated spreading myself. I've always seen every one of
my experiments through to the end.'

Dod's father is on his feet. It is clear he is deeply
disturbed.

'Really...Married...You?'

'Not any more. I exhausted the subject.'

He observes Dod for a moment through half-closed
eyes, making clucking noises with his tongue.

'Your son has a touch of melancholia in his eye and
I don't like it at all. It's high time he was taken in
hand again.' His father protests at this. 'Shut up,
David. You were an excellent chemist and your glyceri
of amidin beat anyone else's. My father used to add it
to all his prescriptions out of pure admiration - and
because he was well aware that the arts survive only
as long as they receive encouragement and support.
But you're no psychologist. Tell me, though, what's
the good Mme Arthème been giving him?'

Dod's father immediately finds the box of phials and
hands it reverently to Dr. Nauser.

'Excellent. I see my diffident instructions are still
being followed. The poor boy must have an arse like
a colander. Still, it's a nice plump one, that's the
main thing. The good Mme Arthème certainly enjoys
her work, and she deserves to, the poor dear.'

'Oh Alexandre, Alexandre,' exclaims Dod's father.
'What a man!' And he wipes his eyes.

'Didn't I put him on haloperidol too, though?'

'I don't remember,' says the father, suddenly anxious.

He is pounced on by Dr. Nauser's loud, penetrating voice: 'But I do remember!'

Dod's father panics. He looks like an old turkey flapping its wings, Dod notices.

'Yes, I believe, er...You're absolutely right, Alexandre. But Mme Arthème...'

'Ah yes, the good Mme Arthème...It did sometimes occur to me to wonder whether she wasn't practising medicine illegally. And why not, for heaven's sake? In a sense she knows as much about it as I do.'

But now there is a knock at the door and Dod's father goes to open it. Simultaneous exclamations burst from him and from another person. He comes back with Dod's uncle. Dr. Nauser clambers to his feet, the uncle walks over to him with arms outspread and the two of them begin slapping each other about the arms and shoulders. After uttering fresh exclamations of surprise and pleasure the three gentle men settle themselves into chairs. They then turn their attention to Dod.

'He's looking fit,' says his uncle.

All three nod their heads.

'And yet, you know, he doesn't go out,' says his father.

'Does he not get taken for a little stroll now and then?'

'In this cold?'

'I've brought him something,' says his uncle, and he places a small parcel secured with an elastic band in Dod's lap.

'Oh you shouldn't have done,' says his father.

'Oh good heavens...' says his uncle.

All three watch Dod as he unwraps the parcel. He takes out a pair of woollen socks.

'Your aunt knitted them,' explains his uncle.

'She spoils him,' says his father. 'But I have a feeling they're a little too big.'

'You think so?' asks his uncle anxiously.

'Maybe not,' says his father.

Dr. Nauser appropriates one of the socks and procee
to examine it closely.

'A very fine pair of socks indeed,' he says. 'The
wool appears to me to be of the highest quality and the
stitch is magnificent. Size is quite immaterial. A
woollen sock can never be too big. On the contrary it
is essential that the end be left free so that it can be
folded back over the toes inside the shoe. Otherwise it
will very soon be full of holes.'

Dod's uncle relaxes.

'Dear old Alexandre,' he says.

'I bumped into him coming out of the station,' says
Dod's father.

'Do you have patients at Sarmes?' asks his uncle.

'Only a little protegee I'd just been to visit,' says
Dr. Nauser.

'Oh, I see - a little protegée,' says the uncle. He
turns to Dod's father. 'A little protegée, is that it?'

Dr. Nauser, with an indulgent smile, says, 'Joseph,
you're talking nonsense.'

But at this point the door opens and Jamyne appears.
She sees the gentlemen sitting around Dod and comes
irresolutely to a halt. Dr. Nauser stands up.

'Do we alarm you, young lady? Ah well, too late.'
And he goes over and shuts the door.

'I popped in to see Dod,' says Jamyne.

Dr. Nauser is already leading her towards the couch
where he makes her sit down beside him.

'So you popped in to see Dod?' he says. 'But you do
the blackguard too much honour. Anyway he has no
time for you: his uncle has just brought him a pair of
woollen socks.'

Jamyne glances at him warily and then tries to
catch Dod's eye. But Dr. Nauser's loud voice booms
out again.

'David, how is it your boy has always attracted the

78

pretty girls? Even at the clinic, a couple of young
nurses I had...He's his father's son, I know, but that
doesn't seem to me entirely to account for it. Could it
be that angelic look...?' He leans towards Jamyne and
whispers in her ear, 'Women have always been intrigued
about the sex of angels...'

Jamyne turns very red. She tugs in vain at her skirt
which has climbed half-way up her thighs and then
presses her knees together.

'Why do you want to hide your legs?' asks Dr.
Nauser. 'They're beautiful legs. I like them very
much.'

Dod's father and uncle are exchanging smiles and
little gestures of complicity.

'Alexandre knows his way around,' observes the
father.

Dr. Nauser has laid a massive hand on Jamyne's
knee.

'So, young lady...What's your name? Jamyne?
Wonderful. Sounds like Yasmina. I once knew a Yemeni
princess by the name of Yasmina a number of years
back. She was a beauty. She didn't have your legs,
though. In fact she didn't have any legs at all. She
used to be carried around on a gold-embroidered
cushion by two black slaves, fine specimens, they
would have appealed to you very much.'

Dod's father and uncle are by now almost choking
with laughter. Jamyne gets up, takes a step towards
Dod, stops disconcertedly and turns to Dr. Nauser.

'I must be going,' she says.

With his arms along the back of the sofa, his legs
stretched out almost straight in front of him and his
head cocked on his shoulder as if to complete this
posture of nonchalant crucifixion, Dr. Nauser surveys
her through half-closed eyes.

'And why must you be going, my child?'

He turns towards Dod's father and uncle and explains.

'Bank holidays,' he says, 'all these young people

leave town with their families or go for an outing, whether it be for pleasure or for the purposes of instruction. But this lovely child, we as yet know not why, has stayed behind, the only creature of her kind in the desert of Sarmes, and as you see she is reduced to seeking some distraction in the company of Dod, a boy who despite his many qualities is as dull as a rainy day. Shut up, David, your son bores me and you can be sure I shall take steps to make him more amusing.'

Then suddenly he stiffens. Old Lousine has started moving about above them. The brisk taps of her walking-stick on the floor fall into groups of varying lengths separated by pauses of a few seconds. Dod fancies he recognizes the series: eight, nine, seven, two, nine. He lets out a sigh and relaxes in his chair. Dr. Nauser is leaning forward, grasping the edge of the couch as if he were about to leap up, listening intently. Jamyne's gaze travels from one to the other with intense curiosity.

Finally the tapping ceases. Each begins to emerge from his immobility, shifting his position, moving his head and casting furtive glances around him like someone in a cinema when the lights go up.

'What was that?' growls Dr. Nauser.

Dod bursts out laughing.

'Shut up, you little fool!' He turns furiously to Dod's father. 'David, what was that all about?'

'Good Lord, Alexandre...It's nothing, I assure you.. It's only an old woman who lives in the room above. She's more or less crippled, at least so I believe, and can only get about with the help of a walking-stick. Really I don't see why...'

Dr. Nauser falshes him a gracious smile.

'Fine, fine, take it easy, dear old friend. But I'm afraid in the long run a noise like that could have a disastrous effect on this young man's nerves.'

He stands up and takes his coat. 'The charming Jamyne will of course dine with us.' Before she can protest he goes on: 'I perfectly appreciate your scruples. These gentlemen too appreciate your scruples. But did you seriously think that the gentlemen and I were going to abandon you in your distress?'

Dod's father and Uncle Joseph are already buttoning their overcoats, chuckling as they do so. Jamyne throws a desperate look in Dod's direction, then turns to the two men as if expecting them to come to her assistance. But they shuffle their feet impatiently, standing there shoulder to shoulder, or exchange rapid whispers while holding one another by the arm.

Dr. Nauser bends towards Jamyne. 'I know a little place down in the harbour district which is great fun. Jolly company and the food is good...'

He is ushering everyone towards the door. All Dod can see is his broad back; he has the impression that Jamyne, his father and his uncle have been conjured away. 'A speciality of this tavern,' the doctor is saying, 'is their goose with sauerkraut stuffing. Sublime...'

Just before closing the door Dr. Nauser passes his head through the gap for a last look at Dod.

'Be a good boy. I'm sure you have a nice book you can reach.'

'I see so many people,' Amalia was saying, when a waiter came up and began whispering in her ear. She darted a rapid glance to one side and gave a nod of assent. Immediately the waiter moved away. Dod followed the direction of her glance. The three gentlemen were sitting stiffly upright and looking towards them. As Amalia slipped down from her stool he thought he detected a flicker of triumph in the eyes of the man who bore such a strange resemblance to his old maths master but who was probably nothing but a simple bank-clerk soured by years of subordination.

'Good-bye,' said Amalia. 'I hope I'll see you again.'

She walked over to the table and the three gentlemen stood up simultaneously to offer her a seat. The waiter arrived with a fresh bottle of champagne.

Dod shrugged. He decided to find the incident amusing and fell into a gloomy reverie. Finally he said to himself there was nothing for it but to pay for the drinks and go home. But he didn't move. He was angry at being a prey to such a ridiculous feeling of frustration and for a moment he considered sitting down at a table, ordering a bottle of champagne and dispatching the waiter to fetch Amalia. The idea had its farcical side and it made him smile. Immediately he relaxed, gave a sigh of contentment and began eagerly to examine his surroundings.

The place was very much to his liking. People seemed to be having a really good time. The faces round him were gay, lively and pleasantly flushed with

82

drink. The women's eyes sparkled, their hair shone
with a burnished gleam, and sometimes, peering
between the moving shadows, it was as if he saw into
the depths of a tropical forest, scene of some carnival
of the birds set amidst a rich profusion of blooms and
lazing panthers... Somewhere off in the deepest
shadows the phoenix was eternally rising from its ashes.

Dod felt like getting up and wandering about among
the tables, speaking to people he didn't know, creating
an affable and sympathetic impression. The barman was
watching him so he beckoned him over and asked in a
ludicrously diffuse manner for another whisky. He
felt a need to spend this wealth of well-being in a flood
of superfluous words. The barman showed not the
least surprise. He was young and had a pleasant face.

Dod felt drowsy. The noise in the tavern was gradually
lulling him to sleep. He had a confused idea that he
would be better off going home to bed but, unable to
make up his mind to do so, he was taking care to avoid
the least movement that might disturb his sense of
well-being... when the explosion of a broken glass woke
him with a start. He found himself looking straight at
the barman, blushed, and said he wished to pay.

His legs felt shaky as he stood up. Amalia had
disappeared and the three gentlemen were staring
glumly at the empty champagne bottle floating in the
ice-bucket. Then Dod became aware that instead of
heading for the exit he was making towards the back
of the room. At that precise moment a voice shouted
his name. He halted, not yet certain. But there was
no doubt about it, someone was calling him. Dod
became as it were the plaything of that mocking voice
which seemed to come now from one direction, now
from another, and mischievously, whichever way he
turned, always rang out behind him. He began to have
a sickening feeling that the mist through which he was
moving was becoming thicker and thicker and he told

himself he was drunk. At last it occurred to him to look up. Overlooking the room was a gallery which Dod was astonished not to have noticed before. Kell, surrounded by a crowd of laughing faces, was shouting and waving to him to come up.

Dod was wide awake now. Eager and greedy for pleasure, he plunged gaily off in search of the stairs that led to the gallery. Kell and the others were all yelling simultaneously. Their instructions were incomprehensible but since the racket they were making was clearly going to start drawing attention to him before very long Dod hastened to put an end to it by setting off in the direction in which they were pointing. Near the cubicles at the back he found a door which opened into a narrow, dimly lit passage. Puzzled, Dod started down it.

After a few yards the passage turned a corner and beyond that there was another door standing ajar. A blast of cold air reached him at the same time as a murmur of voices which the din from the tavern was now too muffled to drown. Vaguely intrigued, Dod drew nearer. The door gave onto a dark alley of gleaming paving-stones. As his eyes became used to the darkness he picked out the silhouettes of two women and a mis-shapen, dwarfish figure standing a little to one side, the mere sight of which made his heart start pounding. One of the women was Amalia. The other was wrapped in a cloak such as nurses wear, her face partly concealed by a head-scarf. They were talking too quietly for him to be able to make out what they were saying. Abruptly the stranger walked off with the dwarf trotting at her heels. Amalia had already turned towards the door and Dod lost no time in retracing his steps back to the tavern.

A waiter showed him the staircase leading to the gallery.

Dod had come to a halt with his foot on the bottom step.

He turned quickly round. Amalia was crossing the room but he gave her no more than a fleeting glance; his gaze went straight to one of the cubicles at the back, pinning down at last the image which had been hovering on the edge of his consciousness for several minutes, had slyly accompanied him all the way along the passage - but then his chief concern had been to find Kell and his cronies - out to the gleaming paving-stones of the alley where two women were whispering together under the anxious and watchful eye of a demonic familiar... How deeply that sight had disturbed him. But now he forgot everything, both the strange meeting he had chanced upon and the cheerful company he had been seeking to join, as soon as he set foot on the bottom step of the staircase leading to the gallery - something had finally caught up with him, something had made him stop, turn round... His gaze went straight to one of the cubicles at the back - and he saw why.

After a moment's hesitation Dod went over and sat down opposite the solitary man who occupied that table, an empty glass before him, so sunk in thought that he appeared to be unaware of the interest he had occasioned. Dod observed him intently.

'Captain Redstone,' he murmured.

The man looked up.

'Redstone... Tombstone...' He repeated the words several times as if testing their sonorities. Then his gaze, vacant hitherto, very gradually brought itself into focus on Dod.

'Tombstone would be more like it,' he said.

And indeed his voice echoed weirdly in the hubbub all around them, as it would have done in the vaults of a crypt - or was Dod letting himself be carried away by the man's lugubrious appearance?

'A name,' he was saying, ' has to mean something, doesn't it? Isn't that what you think? You come and sit yourself down here, you say Redstone, and you expect... what, exactly? For some glory... vanished

for ever...to blaze again before your very eyes?
Redstone, huh? With all Bengal in his pocket...'

'Captain Redstone, don't you recognize me?'

'Captain Tombstone, at your service. If it's Redstone you want, go and ask the Witch...Devil knows
what she's done with him. I said the Devil...Maybe
she's carrying him round on her finger, set in her
ring...Ah!...'

It might have been a laugh or it might have been a
death-rattle; Dod had never heard a human being produce
a sound so unbelievably harsh.

'Redstone, huh? A tiny little puff of white powder
set in a ring...Ah!'

Dod was about to come to his assistance when, very
calmly, he went on, 'Of course I recognize you, to be
sure. Your name is Zuky. What will you have to drink?
And before Dod could answer he was summoning a
waiter. 'A tomato juice for the gentleman who does
me the honour of...'

Dod opened his mouth to decline the offer and at the
same time establish his identity. Before he could
resolve this tricky problem of expression an imperious
gesture cut him short.

'I know...Zuky's no more your name than Redstone
is mine. But can't you make do with a semblance of
a name, seeing you put up with a semblance of an
existence?'

There was a glint in the man's eye and he was beginning to show signs of a quite unexpected liveliness.
But suddenly his expression changed, and it was with
an anxious face that he leaned towards Dod and asked,
'Brought me any news from yonder?'

Jamyne is whirling round and round in the room, her
arms clasped to her breasts, her head thrown back on
one shoulder, her long neck curving upward in a
fabulous sweep; staring into space, turning, turning,
always anti-clockwise - as if she were trying to wind
back time second by second, it occurs to Dod, though
he draws no conclusions. He notes, as she passes,
minute variations in her speed; an almost imperceptible
slowing down at times, like the tiny aberrations of a
heavenly body. He is a little annoyed that she is not in
a better mood. And more particularly he fears that
this whirling round will end by making her dizzy. How
can he stop her, though? He puts his finger-tips to
his temples. After a moment he discovers that his
annoyance is not wholly unpleasurable. The girl's
distress brings a sweetly pathetic quality to the dreamy
grace of her movements, a quality to inspire confidences
and tears.... Oh slow liberation of desire, oh muted
passions and the pangs of deadly caresses! It is
impossible to look upon so vulnerable a creature, Dod
says to himself, without being moved by a desire to
hurt it. Abruptly she comes to a halt in front of him.

'And you,' she says - Dod immediately adopts a
vacant expression but she won't let him escape; she
hems him in and imprisons him with her gaze - 'you
let him do it!'

'I thought you'd have an amusing evening,' he says.
'Dr. Nauser is a very amusing man.'

She opens her mouth but says nothing. Gradually

her annoyance gives way to incredulity. She stares at him as if seeing him for the first time. Then she goes over to the couch and sits down, her back straight and her hands on her knees. Pleased, Dod gives her a friendly look.

'All things considered,' he says, 'you had a pleasant enough time.'

'I slept with him,' she says.

Dod places a finger on his temple and checks the pulse of the artery. It is still quite gentle. If he could rest, he says to himself, even for as little as half an hour, there would be a slight chance of his avoiding an attack of migraine. He further tells himself that he must remember next time to ask Dr. Nauser for a new cure; there is always a new cure and perhaps at last, he will find one that works.

'What about Uncle Joseph,' he says, 'and my father..

'Why? Would you like me to have slept with your Uncle Joseph and your father too?'

'I mean while you were...'

'While I was making love with Dr. Nauser?'

She muses for a moment.

'He's quite at home, there, in that tavern. A girl who works there lent him her room and then went back to keep your Uncle Joseph and your father company. I don't think it's the first time she's done him that little service.'

'I'm glad you had a nice evening,' he says.

Jamyne's eyes fill with tears.

'Why did you let me go with him?'

'I had a headache,' he says. And he touches his temple again. Jamyne's mood will change before long. He wishes it would. Usually they talk about pleasant, easy, transparent things together and their conversation is like the play of light and shade on the surface of a shallow lake - barely disturbed by the occasional furtive emotions which Jamyne's beauty arouses in him, thereby heightening his pleasure.

88

'He treats you like a child,' she says, 'or a simpleton. And he may be right. Perhaps you are only a child or a simpleton.'

'I'm only an invalid,' he says with a smile.

'I'm sorry,' she says.

He sees she is overcome with tenderness and he quickly throws out: 'In short, then, you carried out an interesting experiment. What are you complaining about?'

But she, with unexpected calmness, says, 'I wasn't carrying out any experiment. I slept with a man and, yes, all things considered, I enjoyed it. If anyone was carrying out an experiment I can assure you it wasn't me.'

She seems to become immersed in some difficult thought.

'I wonder...Deep down...Because I was only a card, wasn't I...Yes, I wonder...what sort of game you think you're playing with Dr. Nauser..'

'You're being too clever,' Dod remarks cheerfully. 'Dr. Nauser is my favourite doctor. It's a family tradition - there's always been a Dr. Nauser to look after us.'

'That man is evil,' she says.

'Evil... No, he certainly isn't that...'

He tries to explain: 'It's just that he exists more than other people...'

Evil can only be measured according to the degree of existence. He examines this idea, turns it over in his mind, finds it without interest and drops it. So it is, he observes to himself, that one launches into irrelevant conversations on no matter what subject, and try as one may to explain things one only obscures them the more.

'At the tavern,' says Jamyne, 'there was a whole crowd of people I knew - Kell, Malou and others. I could see them cackling to themselves...'

Suddenly she assumes a curiously sly expression

which is so little in keeping with her child-like features
as to give the impression that she is sending up a part
in an old-fashioned melodrama.

'Do you know what Olivier says about you? He says
that you're a shammer. That you're pretence made
man. He says you've never really been paralyzed -
at least, you weren't at the beginning. The paralysis
set in later. He says that one day you just decided not
to walk any more and pretended to be ill, setting yourself a certain period, because you were never afraid of
an experiment or because, as I understand it, there
was something you couldn't have, just like a child, and
so you chose a roundabout method of getting your way,
but that you pretended so successfully that the illness
became your true nature and that you'd like to be able
to walk now but can't any more because you're hoist
with your own petard. At least, that's what Olivier
says.'

She stops, vaguely scared at what she has said.

'Olivier was always a great man for a theory,'
replies Dod sententiously.

'He told me a lot more, too,' continues Jamyne,
recovering her nerve. 'He says you used to steal drugs
from your father's shop and try them out on yourself to
give yourself special powers, and that you even tried
to make him take some but he refused. These drugs -
I'm telling you what Olivier told me and he talks too
cleverly for me to understand everything he says -
these drugs apparently broke down the resistance of
your nervous system to the point where a simple
affective shock was all it needed to knock you out - but
you'll have to explain to me what he means by an
affective shock - and that that's when you retreated into
your illness.'

'Is that all Olivier told you?'

Jamyne shrugs. 'I didn't feel I had to believe him.'

Dod gives her an indulgent look.

'I know exactly how you feel,' he says. 'But when

90

you get to know Olivier well...He's a clever chap, not
entirely devoid of intuition, but much too romantic for
one to be able to trust to everything he says. And to
return the confidence I've always felt that my existence
was something of an embarrassment to him - no really,
I know it sounds unlikely, but it's the simple truth -
my existence embarrasses him because it fails to
conform with that of the fictional character he's always
trying to create in my place. And do you know, if I
didn't watch out, this imaginary person of Olivier's -
poor old Olivier, basically he's just a kind of Sancho
Panzo dreaming up a Don Quixote to have the adventures
he's too frightened to have himself - well, it wouldn't
be long before this person supplanted me and started
indulging in heaven knows what unspeakable escapades
for which I would naturally be held responsible. You
can see the kind of complications I avoid. '

'You're making fun of me,' says Jamyne, 'and
probably I deserve it. I wonder now whether you aren't
both in league with each other, Olivier and you. It
wouldn't be the first time you've both had me on. '

Dod is cheering up considerably.

'You're like Olivier, love - a brilliant imagination
riding roughshod over logic. But it's what makes you
so attractive and I'm very fond of you both. '

He stops speaking, all expression drained from his
face, as if abandoning the attempt to continue an effort
which is too much for him; he is pale with exhaustion
and boredom; the door opens with interminable slowness
and his mother enters the room.

Jamyne leaps awkwardly to her feet and stands there
with an uncertain smile on her face. His mother looks
sour. It is the third time she has found this girl whose
legs are too long and whose skirts too short here. Dod
can understand her not being particularly pleased to
see her. They both remain motionless, each waiting
for the other to provide a lead. Jamyne, the more
sensitive of the two, looks at her watch and exclaims,

'Heavens, look at the time! I must be going...' His
mother gives a nod of approval - 'I do hope it's not
me chasing you away?' - and turns her back on the
girl.

As soon as the door has closed his mother sits
down, spending a considerable time arranging the folds
of her skirt. Dod says something but his words are
engulfed in the immemorial silence which falls between
them whenever his mother is not in a mood to talk.
He watches her for a moment but what he sees only
arouses in him the usual tedious reflections, so he
turns to the window and sinks into another kind of
absence...All this, said Apollonius, has no reality
but is pretence, and your delicate and lovely wife is
not a human being but a vampire, a lamia. And the
vessels of gold and silver disappeared, the delectable
dishes vanished, the attendants crumbled to dust, and
the haughtily beautiful lady became a hideous ghost...

'...All this,' Captain Redstone was saying, 'has no
reality. The Witch makes us see what she wants us to
see..Our visions are the whims of the Witch...all
these festivities through which we pass, and other
phantasmagoria...'

He cast a wary glance about him, lowered his voice,
and with a look of childish guile and terror said, 'I
pretend to be duped...But I know. Oh, I know all right
young man. Oh yes...And paid dear for the knowledge.
Look at me...and allow that all the treasures of the
Queen of Sheba wouldn't redeem the price I've paid.'

There he sat, this devastated being, like a cinder
with still a spark of life left in it, doleful, venerable,
an empty glass on the table before him, now toying
with madness, now her gloomy plaything, monarch
and jester cohabiting in the one man. Suddenly his
fingers closed round Dod's wrist.

'She's watching us...Quick, let's look as if we're
swopping small talk...'

And instantly he adopted a haggard expression

which was evidently intended to suggest an air of nonchalant merriment. Dod, glancing out of the corner of his eye, saw Amalia standing a few feet from their table; she appeared to be carrying on a lively conversation with the three or four rowdy and somewhat inebriated men sitting there - one of them had taken hold of her bare arm above the elbow - but it was obvious she was looking in their direction.

'Is she the Witch?' he asked in an undertone.

Redstone immediately snapped out of his childish play-acting.

'Her?' He gave a hoot of laughter. 'My dear young fellow, you've had a bit too much to drink.'

The remark was all the more irritating for the fact that he had been brought nothing to drink whatsoever.

'You're joking, of course,' went on Redstone. 'Her - ye gods! She's just one of the servants.' He leaned towards Dod. 'You'd be wrong to underestimate her, though...I can even see the thread she's got you by. What the mistress scorns, the servants scoff, eh? Isn't that it?'

'Do I know this mistress, I wonder?' asked Dod with a smile. 'Let me guess. Would her name by any chance begin with M, such as...'

'Mary,' breathed the old man.

'...such as Mabel? I'm so sorry, Captain Redstone, I should have asked long ago after Mrs. Mabel Crocker-Jones. If you knew how dear her memory is to me...'

Redstone shrugged and gave him a pitying look.

'I don't doubt the excellence of the memories you have of her...I mean the Witch, the one who used to be known as Morgana and whom you might equally well know as Mary Seymour...She has the power to leave you with the clearest memories of things you have never seen and of all that has never taken place...Not that she may not later produce the people and events you remember.' He froze in an attitude of what appeared to be intense concentration. 'Can't do it to me,' he said at last, in an utterly fraudulent tone of voice.

But Dod was no longer listening. A name had escaped those raving lips and the din of the tavern had faded into the background, just as it had when he had passed through the door - after a few yards the passage turned a corner and beyond that two women had been discussing his fate in an alley of gleaming paving-stones - he could still hear Captain Redstone's voice and it tallied eerily with the indistinct words that had been spoken there, tallied too with that other, earlier voice whispering into his heart ambiguous promises of a happiness that was ineluctable. Then he had a sensation of being short of breath, of making futile efforts to breathe in this vacuum through which he was falling as someone said over and over in his ear, 'All this has no reality...'

The landscape has been restored to its essential insignificance. A retreat has been made into greyness. Just a landmark left here and there against an improbab future. But in any case it is to be expected that soon nothing will be left, for winter has no memory: one of the fifteen-storey tower-blocks has already disappeared and Dod can see the end of the right wing of the New University. He notes the fact with indifference, in the grip of the familiar anguish, but what a relief to have reached the lowest level at last, to have finished falling, at last, having been falling from the moment of opening the eyes...At last to have reached the misty depths, to rest, lie down, partake of the greyness, become lichen, mildew, minute lichenous pain, clutching at no more than a blob of ooze now, the ooze still throbbing yes, probably, but so weakly, the mean, beggarly anguish of life's last gasp...and above all to know that night will soon bury even that.

His mother is sitting there, coming gently to the boil. Suddenly she says, 'I've had a most surprising letter from M. Ruck, your Latin master...'

Dod says to himself that his mother is always
receiving letters which prey on her mind. She is already
rummaging in her bag, but she finds nothing.

'How very annoying,' she says. 'I must have left it...'

She purses her lips, subjecting Dod to a precise
scrutiny.

'Never mind...' She pauses, selecting her words.
'Poor M. Ruck...He's deeply disturbed about some
improbable news he has received from...You remember
M. Vitarque, your maths master in the fifth form...
Yes, that's right, the fifth form. I believe you probably
do remember the good man because he bore a grudge
against you for a long time after that naughty joke you
played on him, a joke in rather bad taste, you must
admit, and which might have cost you dearly if it
hadn't been for your excellent marks. Good gracious,
what a business! You - putting a toad in the chalk-box!
I always thought Olvier was behind it somehow, it was
just the sort of thing he'd do, and I wouldn't be at all
surprised if you owned up instead of him. Well,
Vitarque - so M. Ruck tells me in this letter I very
much wanted to read to you - Vitarque has just been
transferred here, to St. Athanasius' College in the old
town...'

Then, speaking more slowly, watching carefully for
the effect of her words on her son, she continues,
'Vitarque knows about the close relationship we have
kept up with M. Ruck and that's why he wrote to him,
hoping he would pass the information on to me, as
indeed he did. The whole story, by the way, as you'll
see, is utterly preposterous. This man apparently
saw you late at night and in dubious company in a
certain establishment in the harbour district where it
is his opinion no well-educated and studious young
man ought ever to set foot.'

She stops, waiting for his reaction, but Dod, with
the vacant stare and drawn features provoked by
migraine, affects the gentle resignation of a sorrowful

son. She gives a shrug.

'The poor man no doubt allowed himself to be taken in by a likeness. That's what M. Ruck thinks too. He is perfectly well aware that you're in no position to go frequenting unsavoury haunts at night, but he thought that in any case it was his duty to let me know.'

She smiles benignly. 'People are funny,' she adds. And yet there is an element of suspicion in her look.

NOCTURNE

A short story by Olivier based
on a narrative by Dod

At the edge of the Park are some clumps of woodland
that once formed part of the old du Theil estate. Few
people venture there, for reasons which are unclear,
but should your evening stroll chance to take you in
that direction you will find, set against a curtain of
acacia trees where the landscape gardener left it, a
marble statue executed in the classical manner. The
single surviving talarium may lead you to infer that
this youthful figure represents - albeit with such un-
wonted whimsicality as to perpetuate an element of
doubt - twilight Mercury. The figure's posture on its
plinth, with body leaning slightly forwards and one knee
flexed, would seem to point to the start of a race, to
the spring that will set him on his way. But a slight
torsion of the body towards the right, the fact the left
hand is raised in a languid movement of the whole arm
up to eye-level with the digits, from little finger to
thumb, spread out evenly to form a perfect fan, and
above all the nonchalant, sensual grace with which the
cheek is brought almost into contact with the shoulder -
Narcissus could not have surpassed it for complacency -
refute this deceptive attitude of flight, introduce a note
of ambiguity, and leave the impression of a creature
alert to obey from moment to moment the conflicting
impulses of a fickle spirit.

To this spot Dod's ambulatory humour one night led
his steps. He saw, by the light of the moon, that someone had come there before him, a very tall man whose
immobility matched that of the statue beside which he

stood with folded arms, plunged, so it appeared, in profound meditation. A broad-brimmed hat cast a shadow over his features. Dod halted, uncertain how to behave and afraid of disturbing the thoughts of this watcher in the deep, melancholy solitude of night. At the same time, however, he was not unaffected by the ostentatious theatricality of such an apparition at that hour and in that place beneath the most perfect moonlight ever to conjure up the phantoms of a park.

The man abruptly emerged from his immobility. With a gesture as of welcome he nodded three times, indicating some mysterious approbation. Drawing nearer, Dod saw that the man was very old; his hands shook and from time to time his whole body would tremble at some colder blast of the night wind. But his grip as he seized Dod's arm was surprisingly powerful.

'I remember,' he said.

The old man's voice was uncannily deep and did nothing to dispel the lugubrious impression created by his manner, appearance and trembling movements and still further reinforced by the circumstances of their meeting, though it would have been impossible to imagine this as taking place at any other time than at night and in any more likely spot than where they found themselves.

'I remember,' he said, 'but each day age makes my memory weaker. Some days, even, I remember nothi. at all, and then, oh the agony of it... I lean over a black hole and at the bottom is an indistinct something beckoning to me.' Then, his tone becoming more confidential, he went on: 'Do you not find this image expresses perfectly the torments of a man suffering from amnesia?'

Dod said that indeed the image did express perfectl the anxieties caused by a deficient memory. He forgo things himself sometimes, certain details, faces, words - of which he probably exaggerated the importa but the feeling was none the less unpleasant, prompting yet another admission of the frailty of human nature and providing yet another taste of the vapid fruits of humility.

'Don't get me wrong,' said the old man, 'I forget everything. I'm like an actor on an empty stage; the theatre is deserted, he no longer knows why he is there, he opens his mouth and says "Oh!" or "Ah!" and his voice comes back at him with such threatening power and charged with such solemn warning that he is afraid to go on. Am I still alive?'

Hardly had he spoken these words than his head appeared to come loose from his body, so sharply did it drop to his chest. Just so will a man who is over-taken by sleep while in a sitting position suddenly stab downwards with his nose. At the same time the old man uttered an incredibly raucous cry which was half death-rattle and half sob. He shot Dod a look out of the corner of his eye to measure his effect before continuing: 'A shade among the shades wandering through these ruins...'

The oratorical gentleman placed a hand on Dod's shoulder.

'Don't, I beseech you take offence. I feel the keenest sympathy towards you and should be distressed were you to take my words amiss. But you must con-fess that it is extremely hard for me to believe in your reality. Besides,' he went on shrewdly, 'one is always the shade of something else. It would thus be a particularly fruitless exercise, would it not, to attempt to impose a hierarchy upon the appearances which act upon the retina, and presumptuous in the extreme to assert: this exists more than that. This world is a world in motion, seat of incessant fluctuations, inexplicable changes of level. Who dare place any confidence in the permanency of the plane which for the time being he occupies? I who have known order and stability find that the memory of the way things were, in so far as I remember it, makes

me sceptical with regard to the phantasmagoria of
the present.'

He raised his hat, revealing a bare and freckled
pate, bowed formally and said, 'I am Baron du Theil.'

Dod made known to him how greatly he valued their
meeting and assured him of the interest with which he
had followed his conversation; indeed he had not failed
to be deeply impressed by the baron's brilliant insights
alike on the theatre, on the physiology of optics and on
geodesy, and was fully cognizant of the advantage he
might draw from them in subsequent private reflection.
The old man bowed once more and said that nothing
could please him more than that a cultured young man
who was keen to increase his store of knowledge should
lend attention to his words. The bluish glint of a
space-ship crossed the sky and the spell of the night
was upon them.

Dod emerged from his reverie to find the old man
talking about fresh-water salmon-fishing. He wondered
what would be the best way to take his leave of this sad
and garrulous character who was rather too gloomy for
his liking and who smelled, as he now realized, strong
of cellars. After a while he caught him saying: 'As for
the shapeless pile known as the château, it possessed
nothing to lure the eye save the signal unloveliness of
its proportions. And yet the flickering light of memor
passing through a ruined brain is enough to annihilate
everything built by your dreams. How do you explain
this phenomenon?'

Dod ventured to reply that it made him dizzy enough
heaven knows, just thinking about it, and that he would
not push presumption so far as to risk an explanation
particularly at such an advanced hour of the night. He
was rejoicing at having found such an ingenious intro-
duction to taking his leave when the baron suddenly
snapped his fingers.

'But I must tell you of our feasts,' he said enthusia
cally.

And so he began to do. He spoke of them in frenzied and feverish tones, in the growing dimness of his poor disordered wits, in jubilation at having lost all reason for living, at having suffered beyond the reach of human consolation. He spoke of them with senile excitation, with outbursts of laughter and sobbing, comical grimaces, clumsy sweeping gestures, with 'ah's' and 'oh's' and with 'um's' when he lost his way and even with the occasional 'huh!' Had a whole zoo awakened in the night amid the howling and the shrieking of captured beasts mourning their native jungle, a whole menagerie in the grip of overwhelming anguish and sick with incomprehension, it could certainly not have wrung your heart with greater vehemence.

On and on the baron talked - of coloured lanterns in the trees, of boatloads of musicians gliding over the lake, of masked figures pursuing pleasure down tree-lined paths deep into the woods...He shrank from no absurdity, balked no fatuity; all the inane hocus-pocus of the fête galante was passed under review.

'Devilish sharp and witty we were, young man, I can tell you - beyond your power to imagine. Ah! I warrant you'll never know the fun we used to have!'

And off he went again, laughing and sobbing more lustily than ever, this poor old fool who called himself Baron du Theil but whom Dod had long since recognized as Captain Redstone.

'Ah, the balls we used to have, young man, the bands that used to play...'

He started humming, and there could have been no more disconcerting sound than that funereal drone which he brought up from his very bowels as, wagging his head from side to side and staring vacantly out of half-closed eyes with his arms dangling loosely, he gradually warmed to the music and began to lurch about, lifting first one foot and then the other - it was almost as if what one heard were the creaking and grinding of this hideous rusty contraption teetering in the moonlight.

The vision was unbearable. But already the spright]
old fellow was beginning to blow like a walrus. Dod
shook him first one way and then another and said in a
friendly manner: 'Come on now, pull yourself together,
you've no idea how late it is.' And he started pummell
the old man in the ribs, endeavouring with difficulty to
restrain the dislocated rhythms that still convulsed tha
venerable carcass.

Then there was a sort of stirring in the bushes, a
rustle of leaves and branches, and three huge dogs
sprang out. Three red-eyed mastiffs whose appearanc
alone was sufficient testimony to their anti-social
nature and immunity to blandishment. In a trice the
baron recovered the vigour and agility of his early yout
Pushing Dod aside with such force as sent him crashing
against the plinth of the Mercury, he leapt into the
undergrowth with the mastiffs snapping at his heels.

The sounds of the chase were soon swallowed up by
the night, but for a long time afterwards Dod could hea
the barking of the dogs, coming, as it seemed, now fro
one direction and now from another, as he might have
followed by ear the progress of a distant hunt. 'He cou
be running till dawn...' he said to himself. And he
reflected with satisfaction that the poor old man would
have no more time on his hands, for that night at least,
to bore whoever it might be with his tales of no-time,
his pompous phraseology, his insinuations and crucifie
airs, his perspiring and trembling and his way of looki
at you as if he expected something of you - perhaps no
more than a flicker of understanding in your eye - and
of shaking his head when he realized that you too could
give him nothing.

Dod slowly climbed the staircase to the gallery, preoccupied by that meeting, wondering why he should be,
and succeeding only in further increasing the confusion
which Captain Redstone's remarks had left in his mind.
He reached the top step and was greeted with exclamations
of feigned surprise, but as they squeezed up to make
room for him he detected in their watching eyes, behind
their words and their laughter, beneath all their
effervescent gaiety, another kind of excitement of
which he was undoubtedly the cause, a strange impatience, a kind of nervous restlessness. Trincart
and Malou were there, both in their second year of
pharmacy - he knew them by sight only and treated
them with all the deference due to elders - as well as
Molly, whom he had already met several times in
Kell's company, and Isabelle, a student from Sarmes.
Sitting between the two girls, one arm draped non-
chalantly around each with the calm assurance of
ownership, was Kell. His lips were curved in his
habitual smile but behind the look he directed at Dod
blazed an intense curiosity. Suddenly he sat up.

'And now, ' he said, 'how about telling us where
you've been all this time? We were getting worried
about you, you know. '

Dod began to sketch an evasive gesture but then
abandoned it.

'I bumped into a friend, ' he said. He allowed his
gaze to wander over the room below. Seen from the
gallery, the confusion in which he had been floundering

103

only a few minutes before, far from resolving itself
now that he was looking down on it, appeared to be
trying to close up on itself and shroud people and
objects in one undifferentiated misty mass. From
where he was sitting only one of the cubicles at the
rear, the last one on the left, was visible, and that,
as far as he could make out, was for the moment
unoccupied.

'A friend? You don't say...At the lovely Lady?
But you know, what surprises me is seeing you at the
Lovely Lady.'

Kell turned to the others.

'This astonishing product of the strictest provincial
virtue...Oh yes, it still exists, my children, don't
laugh...'

Once again Dod wondered what could be the reason
for this animosity which, without ever coming out into
the open, imparted by means of suggestion and innuendo
a private meaning to the most harmless of Kell's
remarks, as if in order to maintain between them,
even when they were surrounded by the rowdiest crowd,
a kind of secret complicity, a link. Kell did not like
him, and yet Kell sought out his company - almost
passionately, as it were.

'...And he winds up here, oh shame, oh holy
women hide your eyes, in this haunt of the damned...'

Molly was trying to stifle a laugh against Kell's
shoulder, but the other girl, the student from Sarmes,
was darting furtive glances at Dod and looking embarrassed. It was the kind of thing Kell was very quick
to notice. He threw the girl backwards and kissed her
long and deliberately on the throat. She submitted
passively, as if indifferent, and then closed her eyes.
Dod looked ostentatiously over their heads. On the
wall right behind them was an old and yellowed poster
headed in large black letters:

THE QUEEN OF SHEBA

'Twelve special performances with Mary Seymour and the Anderson Opera Company,' continued the poster in smaller type.

'This friend - it wouldn't by any chance be the one who was keeping you company at the bar, you know who I mean, the friend in the pink dress...?

Trincart and Malou gave great hoots of laughter and set about slapping each other heartily on the back. It dawned on Kell at last that Dod was no longer listening. He turned sharply round, glanced at the poster and smiled.

'If you're feeling like a visit to the theatre,' he said, 'I'd advise you to choose another show. That one was the toast of the fans last year. But I should be delighted to put you in the picture, oh impenitent if neophytic night-prowler, regarding the reason why this poster is displayed here and, by the same token, regarding certain of the mysteries of the Lovely Lady which might otherwise escape your ingenuous notice, if not your wandering hands, because less than an hour ago you and the said mysteries were practically rubbing shoulders, as I call the present honourable company to witness...'

At that moment a kind of ripple passed over the sea of noise filling the tavern; a movement down below drew their attention to the cause of the disturbance. Three or four men had picked up a woman and were holding her in the air at arms' length and carrying her off, with her hair in disorder and her dress half-way up her thighs, amid shouts of laughter and applause. The woman, who was laughing too as she struggled, was Amalia, and Dod recognized her ravishers as the men she had joined near Captain Redstone's cubicle. The group passed out of sight beneath the gallery.

'Well, well,' said Kell, 'if they haven't gone and abducted our friend's latest conquest! Isabelle... Molly, my darlings, come help me console him. Look, old man, this Amalia... Oh yes, there's no need to

make such a face, I know Amalia too, you know...
Who in this delightful establishment does not know
Amalia? She's paid to be known. And you've just
seen for yourself how popular she is. However, take
it from me, don't let yourself be misled by appearances

Under the admiring eyes of Trincart and Malou,
Kell adopted a melodramatically conspiratorial expression; darting a few comically furtive glances to
right and left, and drawing Isabelle and Molly towards
him until their heads were almost touching, he lowered
his voice and went on: 'The Lovely Lady is one of the
pleasantest spots in this splendid and ancient harbour
district; each evening it is filled with peace-loving
citizens, educated and cultured sailors and the more
sensible type of student. People get discreetly canned,
there are no fights, and you'll never see a police raid..
The police aren't stupid - they know they won't find
anything, and even if they should happen to, some high-
up will soon drop a hint to the effect that too much zeal
may damage the career of the ambitious servant of the
state. Take Amalia, now... she's a good girl who
helps you drink your champagne or your beer, dependin
on your means... Believe me, it isn't enough just to
show her your wallet for the conversation immediately
to take a more intimate turn. And yet the Lovely Lady
has a bad reputation. Later on you'll see the randy
looks on the faces of the bold citizens popping in throug
the door; they're disappointed every time but back they
come, patient and docile. Amalia's a good girl...
She's paid to be know, but not too well... maybe. They
say - and there are always people who know the inside
story or claim to - they say that inquisitive and enterprising young lads have been known to disappear
suddenly, probably because they were too inquisitive
and too enterprising, who knows? But after all, what's
so wrong about that? Everyone has his little secrets
and Amalia's secrets are nobody's business but her
own - I'm sure you agree. Mind you, I wouldn't be at

all surprised myself if all the scandal were put about
by the shrewd management of the Lovely Lady to
attract their beastly customers. But others will tell
you it's a matter of only lending to the rich. All the
same one thing might well intrigue the anthropologist
who dropped in to study the local customs, which is
why you and I come here, old friend, isn't it, or did
you have something else in mind? At any rate, as I
was saying, the only thing worthy of note is the quite
astonishing respect which the staff of the Lovely Lady
show towards dear Amalia - one might even go so far
as to use the word deference. You'll observe that one
look from her is enough to bring a waiter running at
the double, positively quivering with eagerness...and
fear.'

Kell smiled at Dod. He was pleased with his
performance. Molly began nibbling at his ear but he
pushed her gently away. His eyes lit up. So great
was his excitment that he was almost trembling. He
bent towards Dod.

'They say plenty of other things too. That Amalia's
little secrets...are not entirely her own. Know what
I mean? And that Amalia's role, important though it
may be, is only of a secondary nature - but at this
point, take it from me, we're getting deeper than ever
into the realm of supposition and conjecture...Talking
costs nothing, though, and we both enjoy exercising our
wits, don't we? All right then, let's not pass the
opportunity. So Amalia, in the last analysis, would
appear to be some kind of go-between...Notice that I
don't say procuress - in fact in this case I'd prefer to
use the word mediator...or even intercessor, Your
finely literate mind will I hope not miss these subtle
linguistic distinctions. Anyway...Go-between - let's
put it like that. But go-between for what? Or whom?
There is talk - and here's where your romantic heart
will start to flutter - there is talk of a mysterious
house out near Les Affanies, and of a woman too...

107

whom you know...'

Very curiously he paused. He gave Trincart and
Malou a cryptic look. Trincart growled irritably,
'...buggar starts you salivating...'

Dod stood up.

'It's not that I'm bored,' he said, 'but I've got a
lecture in the morning...'

'Really?' asked Kell. 'Do my stories not interest
you, then?'

'You'll have plenty of other chances to tell me them.

'Listen, tomorrow...late afternoon, say around five
I'll be in the Dauphin. Meet me there and we'll have a
chat.' Noticing Dod's hesitation he added, 'Anyone
would think there were things you didn't want to hear.'

Dod shrugged. 'Not at all...I'll be there.'

As he came down the stairs from the gallery he saw
that Captain Redstone was still sittting motionless
before his empty glass, staring fixedly in front of him
with his features sagging as if lost in amazement. But
he felt no desire to join him. He was thinking about
Isabelle.

A bright, frosty January morning but, as Isabelle points out, the sun is so beautiful that it would be a great shame not to take Dod over to the University, look how pale he is, and Olivier nods agreement, it's a good three weeks since he last poked his nose out of doors. So it's decided; Dod is wrapped up warmly, and off they go.

The wheelchair bowls briskly through the park over the glittering film of frost while Isabelle and Olivier keep up a continuous stream of bright, whimsical conversation consisting of disconnected remarks, exclamations and bursts of laughter following one another in a rapid rhythm but punctuated from time to time, and this is more noticeable in Isabelle's case, by a slight breathlessness occasioned by the cold. Dod, observing this, is moved, as if the dazzling light had shown him how perishable is this unique moment of youth, as if he were hearing his friends already from another world, and he marvels at their miraculous gaiety.

Isabelle leaves them at the main entrance of the Arts School and runs nimbly up the few steps that constitute, for the wheelchair, an insurmountable barrier. Olivier sets off again with Dod and goes round the building to a door which, because of the difference in levels, takes them straight into the basement. After wandering for a minute or two down deserted corridors he stops, uncertain and embarrassed; he cannot remember the way. He knows, he says, that there's a lift somewhere over in that direction and he thinks the best thing would

be for him to go off in search of it alone without
involving Dod in any further peregrinations. Dod
agrees. No, he doesn't mind. Why should it bother
him? He's not a child, he can perfectly well wait there
until Olivier comes back to fetch him after he's found
the lift. Yes, it's a real maze with all these corridors,
isn't it? He'd never have believed, he adds with a
laugh, that the basement of an Arts School would be so
elaborate. He'll use the wait to read up his notes from
the last lecture.

Dod listens to the echo of Olivier's steps as he
walks away down a side-corridor. Then, abruptly,
something swallows them up. A stupendous silence
falls. Vainly Dod tries to keep his mind on the text he
has set himself to read; time after time he looks up
anxiously, like a frightened horse turning its ears this
way and that, alert to the probable dangers inherent in
being alone in a hostile world.

Olivier has left the chair right in the middle of the
corridor and Dod can see it stretching away before
him farther than the eye can reach, not because of its
length, though this is considerable and is even prolonged by the perspective effect of the water and steam
pipes running along the walls, but because of a sudden
obscurity in the distance, due no doubt to a lighting
fault, creating an area of uncertainty and mystery
which, Dod is convinced, would immediately be dissipat
as soon as one approached it. Once or twice, looking
up, he fancies for a moment that he can see things
moving against the walls, but realizes these are simply
suggestions made by his nerves which are becoming
frayed with waiting and seize any pretext for fabricating
perceptions in a place so lacking in external stimuli.
At any rate he finds the scientific plausibility of this
explanation satisfying. He finally fixes his attention
on the only two objects he can find to look at - a broom
and a bucket which someone has left against one of the
walls.

The broom is of a rudimentary type such as one would not expect to come across in an Arts School, consisting simply of a bundle of twigs fastened to a crudely fashioned pole. It is an extremely primitive instrument and one which is not often seen nowadays. Dod recalls the name still given to such brooms in the few surviving farms around the town where he was born: they are known as besoms. But then he remembers that he did not hear the word until many years after he had discovered, during one of his explorations of his cousins' house, the object to which it referrred, in a deep cupboard on the first floor which, to his great surprise, had contained nothing but this one, single broom. Then, as usually happened, Clotilde had appeared, seized him by the ear and dragged him back downstairs.

The sound of voices rouses him abruptly from his day-dream. It is no more than a whispering, but the echo has caught hold of it and amplified it out of all proportion and is now rolling it around from corridor to corridor in such a way that it is impossible to tell where it comes from. Dod looks up and down his corridor with a mixture of hope and anxiety. And now someone emerges from the next side-corridor but one and stands there frozen in a curious posture fifty feet away from him. Dod sees that it is in fact a couple, a man and a woman wrapped in a close embrace, so close indeed that they might for a moment be taken, the light seeming to stick to the walls and floor and ceiling leaving as it were a kernel of fine mist in the middle of the corridor, that they might, before the eyes became adjusted to the distance, be taken for a single creature, although of a somewhat unusual shape. The whispering has stopped. The man and woman remain for a moment silent and motionless. Then, very slowly, they start to revolve as if performing some exaggeratedly languid waltz, or rather as if they were just launching into the first step of a waltz, just beginning, forever beginning.

111

At each turn Dod catches a momentary glimpse of their faces and he fancies he recognizes Jamyne and Professor Massoret. But with a sudden glide to the right they disappear from view. The whispering resumes, continues for several seconds and terminates in a brief burst of laughter which the accoustics of the basement invest with such a pitiless quality that it is like a row of sharp teeth savaging Dod's soul.

Olivier comes back looking fed up. He explains that he has spent longer looking for Dod than it took him to find the lift. He says this almost spitefully, with a touch of bitterness in his voice, but Dod guesses that really he is blaming himself for the anxiety and help-lessness which his friend must have experienced during minutes of waiting.

They proceed in silence to the lecture-room on the first floor. Mercifully their entrance passes unnoticed, coinciding as it does with that of Professor Massoret, he by the door at the top, they by the little door to the right of the rostrum which is concealed by an angle of the wall from the view of the majority of the occupants of the room. Olivier hesitates for a moment, gives Dod an inquiring glance, mutters, 'You'll be O.K. here duly leaves him there and hurries to occupy a vacant seat in the very top row. The hubbub dies down almost immediately.

Dod, though he can hear the professor, cannot see him. Stuck there against the wall like some unwanted and possibly even indecent object, he reflects that this time Olivier has definitely behaved in an extremely off-hand manner. His field of vision is limited to the last two aisles on the right and - but then only if he leans to one side and cranes his neck painfully - part of the students in the next aisle. In any case he can see no one he knows. To start with he had had all the curious stares of all those tiers of faces rising above him, so many stern court-room faces crushing him into his

incongruous wheelchair, and he had felt an almost
physical sensation of shame bearing down on him. Now
no one is paying any attention to him, they're all
scribbling away, the professor's talking, no one has
either time or inclination, not any more, for idly
musing on his unseemly presence down there in the
corner. Dod, too, tries to take notes, and for the
space of several minutes he genuinely feels he is
following the lecture. Then he becomes aware that
at certain moments the professor's voice is so distant
as to be inaudible, or else it is indistinguishable from
the rustling of the rain - but you know perfectly well
it's not raining - or it very oddly changes tone, becomes
deeper, becomes the voice of Captain Redstone saying,
'You saw her, didn't you boy, tell me, come now, speak
up, tell me, I know you saw her, you did see her,
didn't you, tell me, come on, I know she spoke to you,
listen, tomorrow, don't forget boy, don't forget,
tomorrow, when you see her again, ask her why...'
Dod inhales deeply and presses his finger-tips to his
forehead. It's abnormally hot in this room. Hardly
surprising he nearly succumbed to drowsiness...
Narrowly missed making a laughing-stock of himself!
He mops his brow and neck with his handkerchief. The
others don't seem to be suffering from the heat, though.
They're all scribbling away furiously, not missing a
word, never even looking up, except that one up in the
fifth row there, leaning sideways in his seat, one
elbow on the desk, chin in hand, taking no more than a
brief, casual note every now and then, a smile of
superior wisdom on his lips. Once again Professor
Massoret's voice mingles with the sound of the summer
rain...Dod, in a desperate effort to keep his eyes open,
fixes his attention on the sole being capable of holding
it, that fellow in the fifth row who looks like Kell...
Looks like Kell - how ridiculous! Kell is more handsome, his face is more delicate, this boy has a slightly
asymmetrical face, they really haven't a single feature

in common...not really...And yet...the resemblance..
can't just be one of expression...But what was it Captain
Redstone was saying?

Captain Redstone was silent. He was staring intently
at his empty glass, his face contorted. And Dod recalled
Kell's contorted face, the expression on Kell's face as
the beer dripped down it...And reconstituting the scene
for perhaps the tenth time, for the tenth time he was
brought up short by that incomprehensible gesture,
always with the same puzzlement yet with neither shame
nor regret, just a feeling of surprise amounting to awed
amazement at the sudden and totally unaffected violence
of his reaction.

'Captain Redstone...'

He had to talk to him, tell him everything...But
Redstone, his mind elsewhere, was turning his glass
round and round between thumb and forefinger. Dod
glanced up at the gallery and almost in the same moment
shrugged his shoulders. Kell...After what had happened
in the Dauphin a few hours ago, Kell would probably not
want to risk bumping into him again. Although...
Knowing Kell, could he not with the same degree of
probability envisage his wanting nothing more than to
bring about another meeting in front of witnesses, out
of curiosity or bravado or simply out of a desire for
revenge? And once again Dod went over his arrival at
the Dauphin.

Kell had arranged to meet him there because the place
was well-known to them both, as it was to many of the
students at the School of Pharmacy, who only had to
cover a hundred yards or so before they were in one or
other of the bars around the Place Radegonde, all of
them dark, gloomy spots, quiet or rowdy depending on
the time of day, and who were particularly partial to
three or four little cellars which dispensed a bitter,
viscous and spleeny variety of beer. Dod had spent the
early part of the afternoon in his room re-reading his
notes on the Collected Works of Paracelsus, emerging

at about four o'clock; he had strolled up the Rue du
Bain and, crossing the Bardo canal, lost himself in
what he secretly termed the 'Colonial quarter'. In fact
this was simply a part of the Admiralty district which
extended as far as Les Affanies Park to the north and
along the Quai Saint-Paul to the east - the Quai Saint-
Paul being the continuation of the Quai des Cygnes on
the other side of the Bardo - with the Place Radegonde
to the west and, a little farther on, the University.
But Dod chose to find a certain 'colonial' charm about
it, deriving from the emporiums for exotic foodstuffs
which filled some of its streets with the smell of spices
and from the little shops, many of them below street-
level, where you could buy all the gimcrack trumpery
of Africa and the East but where too you might occasionally
come across some rare and precious piece, the genuine
article, for which you nevertheless found youself paying
a handsome price; but deriving above all from the old
houses with their tall, narrow windows of tiny panes
revealing nothing of the mysteries within, gloomy
dwellings harbouring memories of the wealth of long
ago when proud ships sailed the seven seas to plunder
vast and colourful continents beneath the gilded ensigns
of the conquering merchant.

The small vaulted bar of the Dauphin was as silent
and deserted as the Place Radegonde itself at this late
hour of the afternoon. Such at least was Dod's impression
as his eyes probed the dim interior. He paused on the
bottom step, crinkling his nose against the pungent
smell of beer. Then at length he spotted Kell and Molly.
They were sitting in a corner, quite still. Molly had
her head on Kell's chest and her arms clasped tightly
round him. Kell had adopted a nonchalant pose with
his head turned a little to one side, no doubt to prevent
his companion's hair from tickling his nose. From
where Dod was standing he was more or less in profile,
and yet he was smiling at him. This sideways glance
accentuated the facetious expression he deliberately

adopted whenever he was with a girl. Here in the pale
light filtering through the tiny frosted window-panes it
gave him a look of malevolent watchfulness, as if he
were searching for the weak spot at which to strike -
and were on the point of finding it.

'Sit down,' he said. And only his lips moved.

Molly lifted her head slightly, said a languid hello
and immediately resumed her former pose. She closed
her eyes to indicate her perfect lack of interest in what
might follow, and particularly in people like Dod who
were so inconsiderate as to barge in on such a delightful
tete-a-tete. Kell was still smiling.

'I wouldn't like to intrude too long,' said Dod.

'But you're not intruding at all, is he, Molly? He
does get some funny ideas, old Dod.'

Molly opened her eyes, kissed Kell on the cheek and
again withdrew into the warm shadows of his body. Dod
hunted for wards.

'At the Lovely Lady...'

'Rather fabulous spot, don't you think?' said Kell.
'You'll have a beer, I take it?'

And with his head still turned to one side because of
Molly's hair he launched into a dissertation, backed up
by long research, on the quality of the Dauphin's beer
as compared with the beer served in the Dutchman or in
this, that or the other establishment in the neighbourhood
Dod stared vacantly at the mug of beer that had been
placed before him. He said to himself that he was in
for yet another dose of the effects of Kell's malicious
concern. But just as the latter was introducing a fresh
digression Dod decided to say: 'I thought you had something to tell me.'

Kell look surprised.

'Me? I said we'd have a chat. Well, here we are,
having a chat...' And he began to unbutton the top of
Molly's dress. 'But you're right...Actually...I wonder
if it wouldn't be simpler if you were to...'

For the space of several seconds he devoted all his

116

attention to the little ball of mother-of-pearl, stroking
it between his fingers.

'Yes...You tell me what you want to know.'

'That's what I'm waiting to hear from you. How do
you expect me to know what it is you want to tell me?'

'All right, that'll do. We know each other too well...
Or at least, I know you. Don't forget I went to Le
Bocage too. Well then...Maybe I have the word on
certain things that concern you.'

'Such as...?'

'We weren't in the same year, I know...But did I
ever get sick and tired of eternally hearing about you!'
He waited until the second button was undone before
continuing: 'Dod's done this...Dod's done that...The
exploits of Dod...Dod the magnificent...The fabulous...
Dod hasn't been seen for a week...Where was he? In
the Castle of the Holy Grail, of course. Even if he
was actually at his grandmother's. You see...?
There's too much literature about you. It's unhealthy.
And all those clots drooling with admiration...Like
poor old Olivier...You've not forgotten poor Olivier,
I presume? Hang it all, he was your best friend...
I mean...Your most faithful admirer. Well...just
about...a year ago...Yes, a year ago exactly, my
friend, it was towards the end of October...Just before
his accident...Do you know, I went to see him last
Saturday at Sarmes...In point of fact that's where I
met Isabelle.'

Hearing the name Isabelle, Molly opened her eyes,
tried to sit up, found it too difficult and abandoned the
idea.

'Olivier's a bit browned off with you, you know -
says you let him down with an imperial thump. But
that's not what concerns us here. What we're concerned
with is what he told me last year about you.'

Kell paused for a moment, his hand inside Molly's
dress.

'And about Mary Seymour. I should tell you I wasn't

117

there for the Centenary celebrations. Not my line, you know, memories of school...I'm not a sentimental man. Anyway, not so sentimental as to take a shine to an actress.'

Dod took a sip of beer. He suddenly felt very hot.

'Captain Redstone,' he murmured.

He would have liked to explain to him that very early next morning - his parents thought he was asleep and probably still suffering the effects of the strange illness that had attacked him the previous evening at the theatre he had run to the hotel where the Anderson Opera Company were staying, only to discover that Mary Seymour had already left. And he himself had caught the train less than two hours later, leaving his parents behind on the platform, anxious, unhappy and secretly annoyed about this departure which was in the nature of a flight. But Captain Redstone, his eyes half-closed, was lost in a dream.

Kell had developed at considerable length the idea that it was not unknown for heroes of romance to confuse the Princess of the Holy Grail with a second-rate actress. Then he had proceeded to kiss Molly comprehensively on the mouth while his hand busied itself inside her dress.

'You can imagine, then...when I saw Mary Seymour at the Lovely Lady...Oh, yes, my friend, at the Lovely Lady - she was singing there. Poor thing... Reduced to working the night-club circuit, and in a place like that, such a...Her - the Queen of Sheba! Scandalous, isn't it? I know how you must feel. But the Anderson Opera was right up Queer Street, you see - not surprisingly for a company that was so bad it had to take high-school engagements. And then...the stuff she was singing at the Lovely Lady was terribly out of date. The minute I saw her I thought of you...'

And he pushed the languorous Molly firmly away from him. She opened a pair of startled eyes and then glumly retreated to her corner of the bench.

118

'See what rotten luck you have. It's not three weeks since she finished her engagement at the Lovely Lady. Poor darling, apparently she'd got a new booking, in London. I had meant to mention it to you at the time but...'

He inhaled deeply and noisily as if recovering his breath after a long run. Kell was obviously reluctant to go on. He chewed his lips and looked meditatively at Dod. Then with a slightly twisted smile he said, 'I had designs on her, you see, and you would have been in my way. I was going to tell you about it afterwards. She's still very lovely...And not so unapproachable either, despite what you might think.'

The same curious expression of doubt crossed his face, and once again he paused for a moment.

'Only...there were rather too many stories about her going the rounds, the kind of stories that can fetch you up where you've no wish to go...And I don't like complications. Nor do I like women whose taste runs to fairground freaks like that little abortion who practically never leaves her side.' Kell was almost panting now, as if in some mysterious way he were suffering; even the indifferent apathetic Molly had noticed and was looking at him with concern. 'Possibly you remember him...He was with the Anderson Company too...'

Dod had grabbed his mug of beer and flung the contents in Kell's face. Molly had stood up with a little yelp and was now examining the folds of her dress for traces of liquid. Kell hadn't moved. He was still wearing the same twisted smile, and in his eyes there was a strange expression as if of relief. Little blobs of froth dotted his face and hung in his hair. Dod was fascinated by the infinitesimal movements of the endlessly seething bubbles; he almost thought he could detect the tiny noise they made as they burst.

'I shouldn't have...should I?'

And he tried to catch Captain Redstone's eye. But

Captain Redstone was not looking. Captain Redstone
appeared to be asleep; the whites of his eyes were
showing between half-closed lids and Dod pictured him
squatting at the foot of a tree in Looking-glass Land,
snoring 'fit to blow his head off'...his face the face of
the Red King - and perhaps I'm no more than something
in his dream, here or elsewhere...Unless it was he
that was the sleeper and Redstone the dream.

A conversation which he had the vague feeling he was
following but of which he cannot recall a word ceases
as soon as he opens his eyes. The lecture-room is
empty. The lecture is over. Isabelle is looking at him
with tender concern. There is someone else beside
her, not Olivier, a tall, dark-haired boy with a serious
face framed by a Newgate frill which makes him look
older than he really is. He too is looking at him. Dod
blushes, sick with embarrassment. Isabelle bends
over him.

'How are you feeling? We oughtn't to have brought
you out this morning. It was too cold...'

Dod murmurs, 'I think I must have dozed off.' He
closes his note-book and stares at it awkwardly.

Then, as if reading his thoughts, Isabelle says:
'This is Jean Brondeau. A friend of mine. He came
to fetch me and as Olivier had another engagement...
Jean is just finishing medicine. He's going to do a
diploma in psychotherapy.'

'Glad to make your acquaintance,' said the other,
and his deep, rich voice rang out with an odd solemnity
in the empty lecture-room. 'I've heard a lot about you.
From Isabelle, particularly...She was quite right -
you have a richly promising aura...Rather disturbed,
though - but still, that's normal for someone who hasn't
yet practised the rites. I'm convinced you will soon
be one of us. And I hope it will be my pleasure to
welcome you personally among the adepts.'

Dod is disconcerted. He darts an enquiring glance
at Isabelle but she, her face shining, has eyes only

for her companion.

Timidly she suggests, 'Perhaps he could come to one of our meetings soon, could he? Perhaps on Saturday...'

'At the Cultural Centre? No...I don't think that would be desirable. We're admitting two new brethren and they're going to try their first communication. Our friend might be...rather overwhelmed.'

'That's true...He's so sensitive.'

'It's never a very good thing to skip the preliminaries. But we'll have other opportunities to talk. You can give him some useful preparation yourself...You can be his guide.'

'I'd love to...Although I still feel very much of a beginner myself...'

They continue to talk over Dod's head, and their conversation seems all the more unreal to him and the effort he has to make to follow it all the more painful for the fact that both are subject to the subtle dephasing effect of the first stages of a migraine attack. Suddenly he has the impression that Jean Brondeau's face is endowed with a life of its own - twitching like a horse's flank when flies settle on it, wobbling unstably like a jelly....Only the dilated pupils of the eyes remain strangely fixed.

'Captain Redstone...'

He must at all costs avert that gaze which denied his very existence and existence of everything behind him, and which annihilated him as it passed through him and propagated itself in the emptiness it created as it went, on and on and on as far as the point it had fastened upon and was contemplating with horror and delight. Dod placed a hand on Redstone's arm - at which he gave a start, shut his eyes, opened them again and seemed for a moment to have recognized him for the first time, so affectionate was the look he gave him, so full of aching compassion.

'You're there, Zuky.'

Then a dazed expression came over his face. Dod

got up and took several steps across the room, as it were in spite of himself, as if he were being dragged along by some current without even knowing whethei he should give in to it or do his utmost to break loose, but with his heart racing once more - as the alarm rang out its 'no more time to lose' - and in the same second...the clouding, the cold gripping the limbs, gripping the body that knows, that is numbed by the knowledge that time is lost for ever.

The woman behind whom he had stopped had thrown back her head and all round the table people were roaring with laughter. Her eyes were almost turned up in her head with the strain of looking at him from this position, and her teeth were bared in a smile that, seen upside-down, looked horribly like a rictus. It was the face of a dead woman. Dod turned away. Affecting an air of bored nonchalance he moved over to the bar. Amalia was alone and beside her was a vacant stool.

'Good evening, ' he said, sitting on it.

She smiled and looked at him without saying a word. He had an unpleasant feeling that she already knew what he wanted to say and he hesitated, disconcerted, groping for words. It was she who spoke first, not leaving him time to utter them.

'You've found a friend at the Lovely Lady. '

He could not help marvelling once again at the clever way she had of asking questions without the slightest nuance of interrogation, making them sound like mere statements. Nor did she appear to be particularly interested in the reply and Dod might have concluded that she had simply been making a polite attempt to start a conversation.

'You mean Captain Redstone?'

'A lot of English people come here. '

'Yes..A lot of English people. If I'd told you he was a bishop you would have replied that the Lovely Lady is frequented principally by the clergy. '

'I can't tell what I would have replied.'

He thought he caught a gleam of distant mockery in her eyes. She was casually showing him the childish nature of his aggressiveness without even condescending to appear surprised at it. He blushed. The...He searched for some cutting epithet, then gave a sigh, suddenly nauseated by his own incurable shallowness and by his hopeless propensity for allowing himself constantly to be led away from the point. Once again he was swamped by the panicky feeling of time running out - the universe teetering on the brink of irreversible chaos...The thing was he needed Amalia. But she did not seem to be in the least prepared to help him, simply watching him struggle and leaving it entirely up to him to break the ice. The silence dragged on between them. Up on their tiny dais the three hungry-looking musicians were playing an old melody he thought he recognized.

'I'm very fond of those old jazz tunes,' he said. 'No one listens to them any more...It's a shame. If you had a good singer, now...'

'People don't come here to listen to music. We keep those musicians more as a favour to them... They're getting rather long in the tooth.'

'You do your bit for charity, I see.'

He clamped his lips shut. What a mess he was making of things!

'Listen...All this roundabout talk is leading nowhere. I know a woman who used to sing here...quite recently. She was English too, as it happens - Mary Seymour...'

Amalia opened a little silk purse and took out a cigarette. Hardly had she placed it between her lips than the man sitting on her right, who had for some time been trying to attract her attention by noisily clearing his throat, making exclamations and passing loud remarks - he had even started actually humming more or less in time to the band, wagging his head from side to side with half-closed eyes and a look of imbecile rapture on his face - than this man offered

123

her the flame of his lighter. He took advantage of
this to engage her in a conversation from which Dod
was immediately excluded.

It had all happened so quickly and Amalia had been
such a willing party to it that Dod suspected her of not
just complying with her professional duties but of
seizing this opportunity to put a stop, for one reason
or another, to his questions. He noticed the barman
eyeing him pensively - no doubt he was trying to convey
with exquisite delicacy the idea that it was hardly proper
to be sitting there when one was too stingy to order a
drink. Disgusted, he slipped down from his stool.
Amalia turned then and said, 'Going so soon?'

And she added, ' Didn't you want to talk to me about
Mary Seymour?'

Isabelle has stopped in the middle of a sentence and
is biting her lips, one thoughtful wrinkle between her
eyebrows. She wants to explain, be convincing...
But there is a suggestion almost of panic in her look.
In explanation after explanation she inevitably comes
up against the inexplicable, or else finds herself
stupidly coming back to where she started from with
no idea how she got there. Patiently she starts again,
and again loses her way; her innocence is disarming,
and all the while Dod feigns an attitude of sympathetic
attention as he pictures her coming naked out of the
water. A respectable girl, she is alarmed to find the
most straightforward statement immediately starts
associating with the lowest company, dodging craftily
about with the shady leer of the logical fallacy. 'Perhaps,'
she adds then, or 'Probably,' her cheeks flushed with
intellectual exertion - so sincere, so beautiful in the
boundless eagerness of the neophyte.

'Jean Brondeau could explain it all to you much better
than I can,' she says at last, giving Dod a look that is
heavy with reproach. She suspects him of being more
or less to blame for the dubious behaviour of her con-
cepts. Summing up her thoughts, she adds, 'You're
rather negative, on the whole.'

'No, no,' he says, smiling. 'I only want to...
What basically are you all aiming at?'

'A higher level of awareness,' she says very quickly.
And with the happy look of the schoolgirl asked about
the lesson she has just been revising - what a piece of

luck - she goes on, 'You see it's principally a
matter of cleansing your perceptions of the deposit left
on them by habit, you have to...as it were transform
your soul and body into a single transparent crystal,
you have to obliterate...yes, that's it, obliterate the
boundaries within which society attempts to contain
the individual, then you enter into communion with
the cosmos...'

'But this is marvellous,' exclaims Dod. 'When do
we start?'

'...?'

'...My soul, your soul and all the world's soul!'

She looks at him for a moment. She is biting her
lip again.

'All right, let's change the subject.'

Dod can see she is very annoyed.

'No, don't let's...'

I'm being too flippant, he says to himself.

'No, on the contrary - I'm afraid I didn't express
myself clearly - I find your...movement...?'

They're after the spirit, obviously. So let's all go
together.

'...Your beliefs, your principles...I find them very
attractive. Although....'

He is always too flippant when he doesn't have a headache, which is how, unintentionally, he hurts his friends
feelings, forgetting in his selfishness to make allowance
for their perfectly legitimate concerns...

'I'm extremely ignorant but I ask only to be taught.
Your Jean Brondeau,' he continues in a non-committal
tone of voice, 'strikes me as a remarkable chap, a
deep, inquiring mind, a sort of Dr. Faustus in the
prime of life, after his rejuvenation, yes...Most
charming. He made a great impression on me.'

'He's wonderful, he's so...'

'...Convinced, isn't that the word?'

'He's a ...'

'...Saint?'

126

'Oh no...A prophet.'

'One always imagines prophets as being rather careless about their appearance, concentrating as they do
on things of the spirit. He is very neat, though.'

'Above all he's free. The police have him under
surveillance. He represents a threat to the established
order. He says the only freedom worth fighting for is
inner freedom, the expansion of human awareness...
It's a question of realizing the full potential of your
genetic code.'

'But that's terrific!'

'During our ceremonies...'

'Be a good girl - pass me my pipe there on the desk,
would you...? No, give me a cigarette instead. You
were saying, during your ceremonies...you communicate,
if I remember our friend's words correctly?'

'Yes..we communicate....But I don't know whether...
I wasn't supposed to tell you about that so soon...Still....'

'Tell me about what, love?'

'About Soma...'

'Flow on, o liquor, all Indra round about!' And,
noticing that Isabelle is looking at him anxiously, he
says to reassure her, 'Just something that came back
to me...But don't stop now that you've gone so far, o
daughter of the Sun, speak to me further of the divine
draught.'

Isabelle's gaze is now clouded with doubt and
suspicion. She shakes her head.

'I don't know...You...Wait, though, I should know...
Olivier....'

'My chronicler...I am forever learning fresh things
about myself merely by listening to the revelations he
makes to others and which they then pass on to me.
You were saying, about Soma...'

'...'

'There...where are granted all of desire's desires...
Instruct me, since to instruct me is your mission.'

'I'm just wondering if there really is anything I can

teach you...I wonder even whether you don't know a great deal more about it than the rest of us...'

'Why? Because I quote from the Rigveda? What does that prove? Nothing...Except that I've read the Rigveda. What of it? It must be out in paperback by now in a translation subsidized by UNESCO. It's culture...And I have the time to read. But my heart is weary of fiction and longs for reality. So - you've discovered the divine secret...'

Isabelle, adorably sly, says, 'There is no secret. Soma is just a symbol for us. Like the bread and wine in the communion service...'

'And more effectual, possibly...But I must say the word symbol seems to me rather inadequate for the practice of such magic.'

'We're looking for something different.'

'Only a god can assuage the hunger of the soul. To which unknown god do you offer sacrifice?'

'Jean Brondeau would say...that you're still clothing youself in the dusty clouts of dead religions.'

'I'm not a modern, that's true.'

'You see...you must first restructure yourself.'

'You're right, I'm tired of my structure. Tell me how I go about it.'

'Start by being modest.'

Dod immediately adopts an attitude of deep humility. 'Go on.'

Isabelle is looking at him with tears in her eyes. 'I remember when I was just starting...But you'll see, you will be wonderfully rewarded. You'll feel you're living a hundred times more fully...You'll discover new and unknown senses...You will become aware of every cell in your body...Jean Brondeau....'

Isabelle is bending over him. He closes his eyes for a moment to breathe in her smell which without being that of honeysuckle is by virtue of some nocturnal association over-poweringly reminiscent of it. He hears her saying, '...At this point you enter the

128

Einsteinian equation.'
    'At this point?'
    'You see, it's one of the principles of the Affanes...'
    'The Affanes?'
    'The Adepts...'
    'But why the Affanes?'
    'It means the same thing.   Jean Brondeau explained
it to me.   In the beginning they used to meet in an old
house in the old part of town near Les Affanies Park...'
    Dod suddenly feels weary.   He has lost interest.
The arrival of Mme Arthème is a pleasant distraction
which he welcomes as the insomniac greets with relief
the surly dawn as it comes at last to blanch his window.
She stares calmly at them both, slowly sizing them up,
giving them to believe that she has guessed, that she
knows, knows more even than they know - her mere
presence bringing to bear on them the reproof which
from time immemorial has accompanied or preceeded
wrong-doing, real or imagined.   Isabelle, flustered,
lowers her eyes.   Her scent of frailty suddenly fills
the room.
    Dod subsides in the voluptuous lap of guilt.

INTERVAL

Several miles out of the town where he was born Dod
had plunged into the woods. After wandering for hours
among the dark trees and the smell of rotting leaves he
came out, towards the end of the afternoon, on to a
deserted road beneath a vast open sky in a part of the
country he did not know. He told himself he was so
late already that it was really not worth hurrying, and
with gay abandon he began kicking a pebble down the
road before him. As far as the eye could see the tall
poplars tossed the wind among their branches.

The first house he came to was set back slightly from
the road, from which it was separated by a white fence.
Beyond the fence was a mass of flowers. Dod drew
nearer. Something warm and tender came out to meet
him, something like a thought, friendly yet alien,
like a distant sound of laughter and whispering that was
suddenly all around him. The door of the house stood
ajar; with a feeling of joy he went in. The limpid
charms of a Dutch interior greeted his eye. He ran
his gaze lingeringly over the flowered Delft, the polished
wood, the copper pots... Then he noticed the child
kneeling on the floor over a picture-book. And just at
that moment a young woman passed by in a sheen of
silk. Her face was lit up as she turned to him: he
thought he saw her smile. He said to himself that he
would never cease to be disconcerted by the unpredictable quality of her movements, and was amused
at the thought for he was seeing her for the first time.
But she was already going away, and the blue of her

dress merged with the blue of the window.

Dod began to speak, struggling desperately to contain by his words something which insisted on escaping between them. Then he found he was alone in the darkening room. A last gleam of copper still testified to the memory of day. The child had taken his picture-book away with him.

He went over to the window. A large bluebottle had settled at the top of one of the panes. She remained still and watchful for several minutes and then cautiously began to make her way downwards. Her path was complicated by little dashes to right and left, sudden about-turns and even short bursts in the opposite direction. When she was on a level with Dod's head she stopped. He was holding his breath. He could distinguish each tiny vein in the transparent wings - and he watched with deathly anguish as his thoughts vanished one by one in those enormous eyes.

Dod turns away from the window and heaves a sigh.
Olivier is still standing there in the middle of the room,
hands in his pockets, his tall body slightly stooped.
Dod would like to say something, give his opinion - he
ought to. He curses himself for not having listened mor
attentively to his friend's confidences. He racks his
brains...What should he say? Olivier, his head on one
side, watches him with his bird-like eye. He is waiting
    'Maybe...'
The transparent absurdity of the advice he was about
to give dissuades Dod from continuing. Olivier's watch
ful gaze is still on him. So he pretends to be thinking.
But in order to show he is thinking he can think of
nothing better to do than examine his nails, and this
annoys him. People are too ready to confide in him,
he reflects bitterly to himself - and I can't do much
else but listen, seeing as I can't get away. The irony
of this reflection calms him down. He goes on to
wonder whether, in the minds of other people, his
immobility doesn't perhaps curiously suggest serenity,
and his impotence become transfigured into renunciatio
and wisdom. Olivier leaves him no time to savour this
comic gem.
    'None of it was true. I've been the victim of a hoax.
And the trap I fell into was laid by no one but myself.
No one but myself.
    He beats his chest deliberately with a bony fist. No
complaints. He tells it, explains it, as if it had all
happened ten years ago. With vast amazement - or is

that shock has thrown him back so far that he now has
this perspective.

'Daft, isn't it?'

Dod sighs and lets his gaze wander outside again.
He looks along the left-hand building, counting, and finds
the window on the fifth floor wide open on a dark and
still empty room. He leans forward as far as he can.
A breath of cold air pushed him back into his chair.
He shivers.

'...Perhaps it started before, in fact it must have
done, I mean it's only logical to assume it did, but it
was on Saturday, at the airport, as I realize now...
Perhaps it happened while I was waiting - and now I
come to think of it, it seems to me I ought to have felt
more impatient. I believe...yes, I was much too calm.
And yet...I'd arrived three-quarters of an hour early.
I couldn't sit at home any longer. But at the airport..
when I looked at the time...being certain I wouldn't
miss her....Strange. I smoked a cigarette, watched
the people, the women particularly, all the young
women, I was interested....I thought about her a bit -
and lots of other things too, even about you, poor old
man. In fact I believe I thought a lot more about you
than I did about her. Every now and then I glanced at
the clock and it seemed a very long time - but I didn't
start feeling excited or anything. As if I'd been waiting
for my uncle - it was a bit like that. Even when her
flight was announced...I saw her coming towards me,
she was smiling at me...Three months we'd been
apart...I ought to have just smiled like her - and
probably I was smiling but at the same time I was seeing
for the first time that she had a nose, a mouth, teeth,
eyes...It was no different from the face I knew but it
wasn't quite the same either. I remember that for the
space of perhaps a second I wasn't sure if it was her.
Imagine yourself one day looking at a portrait and the
next day meeting the model. Something's...not quite
right. You tell yourself the likeness is perfect but

there's something nagging at you... something in the transposition. In short, you don't need the model. On Saturday, worst luck, I met the model. '

Olivier strikes a pose. His round, bird-like eye has not left Dod for an instant. He is clearly going to tell all.

'During the Christmas holidays I saw her every day, often from morning till evening, and evenings we went out together. The hours I spent looking at her - I felt I was learning her face by heart. The fact that she had a nose and mouth, all right, even the shape of her nose and the colour of her eyes - none of that was beyond my powers of observation. I was even aware of the imperfections in her features. I could have given a fairly exact description of her, I think. But there was the transposition. On Saturday her nose, her over-large mouth, the texture of her skin - everything irritated me. I couldn't stop detailing every fault. Maniac that I was... poor, sad, idiotic fool - maso-chistically gathering evidence of the imposture but at the same time quite ready to be dazzled all over again by the palest reflection of... the other person. Suddenly I had an explanation: her hair wasn't done properly. I told her she must change her hair-style. '

Olivier strikes a fresh pose and Dod feels driven to offer his point of view.

'Wasn't that a bit clumsy?'

And that's precisely what is so annoying, says Dod gloomily to himself. One always chimes in with the wrong thing. Better to resign yourself from the outset to playing the bumpkin they're so eager to cast you as. Pointing to a chair he invites Olivier to sit down, but Olivier, still with his hands in his pockets and taking up a firm stance on his slightly parted legs, rattles imperturbably on.

'I believe... inside us... there is a vacuum. A vacuum...' And with is hand he attempts to delineate this absence. 'Nothing fills it, yet everything clutters it up. The funny thing is that we want desperately to lodge something there - something or someone. Uninhabitable, old man. Everything buggers straight off again. Not even time for a house-warming.'

And as he launches into a minute exploration of this allegory, like a ship-wrecked sailor making a tour of the island on which he has been cast up, Dod once more makes his escape. The sunlight is falling at an angle on the facade of the left-hand building, but now a cloud passes overhead, the light dims, and it is like the silence that falls in a room when someone comes in whom nobody knows, and all exchange questioning glances. Within the narrow frame of the eighth window along on the fifth floor a woman has just crossed the dark interior. A fleeting, uncertain vision, but one which is immediately borne out and elaborated by other images, earlier and more precise. Dod recalls, by analogy, leaning out over the river near his home, in one of the shady retreats to which it was his habit to escape during the long lazy afternoons before the departure for Hampshire, and watching, often only a few feet from a dozing fisherman, the evolutions of the fish in the watery depths. He would try as long as he could to follow with his gaze their nonchalant and capricious quest, until with a rapid flick they vanished among the reflections. When he saw them again it was never where he expected to find them, reckoning from what he thought to be the direction of their flight; he was not even sure it was the same fish he was seeing for how was he to identify them from one appearance to the next? This is certainly simpler, watching this narrow rectangle of darkness out of whose depths emerges the image of an indiscernible but at least unique being.

Dod lets his gaze glide where it will over the concrete landscape. The fluctuating March light caresses the facades of the buildings in obedience to the clouds that pass overhead. Down below him the schoolgirl is

skipping along one of the paths with a clever, complicate
movement. Would it be because of the distance? The
sun, already high in the sky, has given her a tiny,
strangely motionless shadow. Dod cannot take his eyes
off the little hopping figure until, abruptly, the silence
makes him look round. Olivier is smiling at him.

'I'm boring you,' he says.

His eyes were misty with tiredness; the noise... The
fearsome jumble of voices seemed to have grown even
more dense and he felt its awful pressure almost to
the point of suffocation. Occasionally a few words
would stand out, prove too absurd to be viable, and
immediately sink back into the mass - words whose
meaning escaped him almost as soon as he had uttered
them, whereupon Kell would look round with an inaudible
mocking laugh, the pitiless witness of his inadequacy -
or he would stop in the middle of a sentence with the
feeling that he had said the same thing before somewhere else, on some other occasion, and it was no
longer Amalia who was sitting opposite him with her
unfathomable gaze but Olivier perhaps, or Redstone;
the captain, braced against all the drink he had taken
in, was sitting incredibly erect on his chair in the
lurid hell of his cubicle. Kell still had the same mug
of beer in front of him but was once more summoning
the waiter, indicating Redstone's empty glass. At that
moment Amalia said something he did not understand;
she stopped the waiter as he passed and she too, though
with no more than a look, told him to bring fresh drinks.
Dod noted with detachment that he was more than a little
drunk. He was amused by the idea that Amalia was
making him drink here - it was her job, after all - at
the same time as, over there in the cubicle, Kell was
relentlessly drenching Captain Redstone in alcohol.
What for? he wondered vaguely. It was clearly one of
those intricate actions whose purpose was beyond

137

discerning - perhaps simply because they had no purpose
but were no more than the perverse and childish express
of a restless mind - one of the actions Kell felt obliged
to perform in order to live up to his part in the play he
was everlastingly acting out, much more for his own
benefit than for the benefit of others. And he had obviously decided he was not going to act out this play
alone but with Dod, to whom he had long ago assigned
a part - such generosity from Kell? - probably even
more important than the one he reserved for himself.
At that point Dod saw him lean towards the old man
and speak to him, his eyes bright with that look of
almost morbid excitement that marked climactic momen
of the play. What could he be talking about? Dod?
Mary Seymour? Amalia too was talking about Mary
Seymour. Like Olivier - who could no longer come to
him - all the hours they'd spent together getting drunk
on the memory of Mary Seymour... All those conversations about nothing but Mary Seymour! And all
mingling in time and space - thousands of conversations
around him, around every table, all those people talking
about Mary Seymour with bright, excited faces, all
those voices building up to one vast, titanic clamour of
Mary Seymour's name! Lord, was he going to do
nothing but let his life run out in conversations?
Nothing but talk about Mary Seymour... Amalia had
caught his look.

'Your friends are great drinkers,' she said, 'the
old sailor especially...'

How long had they been meeting here every evening,
Amalia and he, always at one of the tables near the
cubicles, always within a few feet of Captain Redstone,
and he ignoring them - and yet he could not help being
aware that they were there right beside him, but no
doubt by feigning indifference he wished to convey to
Dod his disapproval - how long had he been asking her
questions every night without ever getting anything...

'That Englishman...'

...except cunningly procrastinating replies?

But the most surprising thing was that he caught himself maintaining a scrupulous ambiguity as if he too were trying to gain time. Gain time?

Mary Seymour was in London, yes, he knew that, Kell had already told him, Amalia was telling him for the second time, she had left for London - and he was positive that she was here. Kell was telling the truth, but Amalia was lying. Mary Seymour was in London, in the ether, in the umbra, here...What did it matter? His destiny was to talk about Mary Seymour, not to meet her. He would always be on the side-lines, on the boundary, too cowardly to cross it. Too cowardly, said the look Kell had fastened on him, a look that blazed with a flame of desperate defiance. Dod offered him a friendly and slightly drunken smile. It felt good to be at the Lovely Lady. There was really no reason to go elsewhere. The Lovely Lady was really the ideal place for talking about Mary Seymour without running any unnecessary risks. The image of a singer who possessed little talent and was already past her prime could, at the Lovely Lady, become adorned with all the most glittering jewels of the Queen of Sheba. So far, in fact, he had played his cards extremely well, allowing his imagination to roam where it would without engendering any damage to his mind. It suited his dilettantish nature. And Amalia agreed. Amalia was an understanding person and despite her distant manner a most affectionate one. She wished him not the slightest harm. That was why she was so careful to maintain between him and Mary Seymour, between the moth and the flame, an adequate and necessary distance. Amalia was someone who must be very fond of moths. She was prepared - and in his heart he thanked her for such clemency - to let him continue indefinitely to sit on the fence between Exile and the Kingdom. For someone with a taste for comfort like himself, the shabby certainties of Exile were greatly preferable to the unknown

perils of the Kingdom. Too cowardly, said Kell's
desperate look. Possibly, but did he not see Redstone
there, sitting opposite? Redstone had done it, he'd
crossed the boundary, he'd forced his way into the
blinding light of the Kingdom, his empty eyes were
proof of that - and where had it got him? Take a look
at him - the old sea-dog moored for good and all at
his rotting berth, the old alchemist, his furnace gone
out for the last time, the old fool, and nothing can
warm him now but the fire of alcohol, is that why you're
plying him with drink - or so that he'll tell you about
Mary Seymour the Witch, her who knows the herbs and
the spells that extol their virtues? But it won't be you,
Kell, who drinks the philtre - or only by means of a
fraudulent third party. Like poor Olivier...back at Le
Bocage. Actually - and Dod was struck with joyful
astonishment - am I not for them simply the Iphigenia
who will allow them to weigh anchor? Waiting at the
foot of the stake for the first breath of wind to send
the dark column of smoke curling into the air... In
any event they wouldn't get far. Kell's most pressing
concern would be to go and beguile some girl into bed
with his caresses and sweet-talk. As for Olivier...
Would he leap to his feet shouting hallelujah, about
time, thank the Lord, but what will Dr. Nauser say?
Yes, that's what Olivier would do - and he would
quickly sit down again. They really take me for
Iphigenia - something of that sort. Under Amalia's
thoughtful gaze Dod smiled and began to feel sorry for
himself, and he told himself he was going to be happy
in spite of Kell's intrigues and silly Olivier's nostalgic
dreams. Poor Olivier...It was a long time now since
he'd abandoned him to his immobility, Kell was right -
the last time he'd been to Sarmes was in spring, he
remembered it....He sat on by the wide-open window,
the fluctuating March light caressing the façades in
obedience to the clouds that passed overhead....

'That window interests you...'

Again Dod shivers and jerks back, and yet the wind has fallen. Olivier is still smiling.

'I wonder, though,' he says, 'whether you really know...'

What Dod is wondering is whether or not to be pleased at this change of subject. It has the advantage of sparing him any more of Olivier's sentimental drivel, but won't that advantage be cancelled - or worse, out-weighed - by the disturbing turn their conversation seems to be on the point of taking? He fears it will. His friend's knowing look certainly augurs badly.

'...who lives in that flat - or is it just chance?'

He says to himself that the trapezoid section of wall determined by his angle of vision is very likely occupied by a mirror - in which, just now, it moved, that shape, that blue shimmer that became the shimmer of a dress, and for a second possibly, he fancied he caught a gleam of blonde hair...

'...Although in your case chance has so far mani-fested, as you must admit, a most suspicious degree of cooperation - not to say complicity. Which, to those on the look-out for it, is the mark of the hero.'

'It goes without saying that you include yourself among the number of those privileged observers.'

'It's the state to which I am reduced, the events of my own life refusing, as you know, to take on that minimum of coherence which is characteristic of a destiny, that is to say the life led by the hero to its glorious or pitiable conclusion. In my prosaically circumstantial existence the lyric breath of adventure is, alas, unknown to blow. '

'And you've observed this curious atmospheric phenomenon in the existence of myself, is that it?'

'While you were struggling to appear attentive to my little problems - I don't blame you, I know whom I'm dealing with...But I had no alternative but to remark that your eyes were as it were glued to the window of Adrienne's room. '

'Adrienne?'

'You don't know Adrienne? Really? How odd... Mind you, I didn't know who Adrienne was myself until Kell told me. '

'Kell...'

'You'll be seeing him again before long. Sarmes, you see, has become the centre of his emotional life. There's Isabelle, and others...'

'Isabelle....'

'He used to be fascinated by you before - you'll remember. He'll want to know all about it, don't worry. Having affairs in Sarmes and knowing this is where you are...Naturally he ran Adrienne to earth straight away. '

'...'

'Mary Seymour's daughter.'

'...'

'Came out of the clouds, eh...? But listen, you must admit Mary Seymour wasn't particularly young any more. And she had a daughter. A grown-up daughter who's now reading law at Sarmes. And who decided to come and live right here - she couldn't get a room in any of the halls of residence - after her mother's divorce. '

'...'

'Don't tell me you didn't know? Mary Seymour and Dr. Nauser were divorced about six months ago now. Dr. Nauser, I might add, has retained a very fatherly affection for Adrienne whom he comes to visit from time to time. He'll end up marrying her as well, the devil! What do you think - ought that to be regarded as incest?'

'...'

'Kell's instinct borders on divination. I mean it would have taken anyone else months to find out... And then there was an element of chance, or luck. Or rather a chain of connected circumstances....Kell called in to see me and came across Isabelle there. Literally, as it happens. Now, Isabelle has just met a new friend, Adrienne... Isabelle, by the way, is rather going to the dogs, did you know? She's got mixed up with a bunch of nuts, a sort of theosophist-cum-drug-addict crowd who call themselves the Adepts. Shame, isn't it? That's how she met Adrienne - she's a sort of cult priestess or something. You begin to see how all this would start making that merry little devil Kell froth at the mouth...He's been quivering with excitement ever since, dashing all over the place making connections, drawing deductions, trying out fresh connections and then rushing to tell me all about it, firmly convinced that everything would reach your ears in the end, and as it turns out he was quite right. But I nearly forgot - there's one thing that may be important, although...Dash it all, I feel a bit awkward mentioning this to you.'

And indeed he does look genuinely embarrassed - he's even started biting his nails. Dod looks at him curiously. Then turns away. Weary all of a sudden. What's the use, he says to himself, he knows, he already knows. Olivier is rehashing as usual. Olivier's everlasting rehash of empty, absurd words, what's the use, he already knows what the fellow's going to say... No, he doesn't know, doesn't want to, isn't interested, anyway how could he know? The conversation bores him.

He leans forward for a glance at that window and

immediately sits back again. He feels cold, he fingers his temple, notes with surprise - with diappointment? - that this time he's not in for a migraine attack; he's just tired, a bit fuddled with so much fresh air after spending all winter indoors, it's quite natural. Dod becomes aware that Olivier is now looking at him - eyeing him, he adds irritably to himself - but his friend's look wavers, evades his own, starts wandering anxiously about the room, poor Olivier, looking for somewhere to dump his huge fluffy mass of ridiculous grief, just about ripe now for a letter to 'problem page', dear Mary, I've just noticed that the girl I love has turned into a frog, I don't like batrachians, what should I do? Poor Olivier, he'll not last out till his death, not long now and he'll vaporize on the spot, turn into a mist, a tiny cloud, a puff of wind will carry him off into the March sky, and yet this incredible lump of peasant flesh...He'll not last out till his death, what does that mean?

'...I even wonder whether it'll mean anything to you now.'

Olivier is talking. That's Olivier's trouble, he talks too much. And when, as now, he becomes totally incoherent, why make the effort to listen? When you're so tired...Mme Arthème wouldn't stand for it, Mme Arthème doesn't like people tiring Dod, she'd be sure to scold Olivier and quite rightly too; everyone's afraid of Mme Arthème with her long needles and her exorcisms Mme Arthème doesn't like hearing talk about Mary Seymour...

'...It was you drew my attention to him, shortly before you were taken ill, just before she came on stage, the little monster in the huge turban with his face painted black...You clutched my arm and you said, I remember your words: Look at that dreadful thing... Then he went and hid behind the skirts of the Queen of Sheba's attendants.'

Dod is suddenly lucid, preternaturally calm. He

says, 'I remember. Go on.'

Olivier stops, confused. He stares at him with anxiety in his face.

'I'm listening.'

'He's here, in Sarmes...'

'Sarmes is like hell: everyone meets up again here.'

'Kell says he's often to be seen at Adrienne's place.'

'Let me tell you something that Kell doesn't know. The little monster's not human - it's just a homuncule that Captain Redstone bred in one of his retorts and gave to Mary Seymour as a present.'

'To Mary Seymour...'

'You doubtless bring me news of the good lady.'

Olivier shakes his head. His great body has never looked so embarrassed.

'I'm sorry...I shouldn't have...'

'Well, go on, talk to me about Mary Seymour - I can see you're quite prepared to replace your own abortive adventure with one that I'm supposed to have had.'

'You arrogant...'

'Me? Here...?'

'Sarmes is like hell, you said. Sarmes is primarily the hell of your arrogance. You couldn't do without.... Living wasn't enough for your exalted character.'

'You talk like a king and I look at you like a cat.'

Then Olivier's image becomes blurred. He hears him add: 'We all fell in love with Mary Seymour...'

A clear liquid reveals nothing of its inner complexity until one drops into it a few grains of white powder, whereupon it becomes cloudy and turgid and a milky hydra begins to form. In the same way space, from appearing to hold no mysteries, will suddenly reject the simple joys of transparency, suddenly precipitate and curdle to an opalescent mass, suddenly start to spark and blaze with the phosphoric fires of migraine. Dod, his forehead damp with sweat, his nostrils pinched, loses all self-assurance. The barriers are down, his

being is open to the sky, risking exposure to the on-
slaughts of the murderous air. Galloping corrosion of
being. Perishing in little bubbles. And then bigger
bubbles. Like those that burst the thick green slime
of a stagnant pool. Demented bubbles...Accelerating,
eddying precipitately into the dark void. Extinction.
Finding oneself slightly to one side. Hovering to one
side. Thinking to one side. No longer quite super-
imposed. Split. A sickening uncertainty about edges.
Agonies of approximativity. Eyes tight shut on a
whirlwind of impalpable downy feathers. Lips pressed
together to avoid choking to death. All obviously useless, shutting one's eyes, pressing one's lips together,
turning one's head, saying to oneself, not saying to
oneself, dithering, ithering, fumbumbling....
Consciousness pillaged by silent hordes. And after the
sack the spectres sit down at cards. The migraine
makes the cards fly faster and faster. The game is
oneself. Brief glimpses of one's bloodless face caught
on each pasteboard square. Then the game thins out.
Gaps appear. Telling oneself one shouldn't drink so
much when one can't take it. And at the same time
knowing one is not drinking. One's joking, of course.
Split. Other. Increasingly other. And in the end
neither this nor that. Between...Between what?
Other. Other. Other...But what was Olivier saying?
We all fell in love with Mary Seymour....Poor Olivier.
Go to Sarmes...one day. Solicitude....

'How pale you are.'

Amalia's hypocritical solicitude. She has placed
her hand on mine. She is looking at me. Anxiously.
Strangely human, all of a sudden.

'Are you unwell?'

Unwell? No more than Captain Redstone sitting so
fantastically stiff and erect over there, bathed regally
in a purple glow.

'You ply me with drink and you ask if I'm unwell?'

Amalia's hand, still tenderly pressing his own, made

146

him angry. He leaned towards her.

'Imagine, we all fell in love with Mary Seymour.'

He had adopted a knowing, drunken look but did not have time to appreciate its effect on Amalia. Behind her a scared-looking creature was darting between the tables. Heads turned and their expressions hovered between amusement and uneasiness. The creature was now passing along the row of cubicles with a strange, crooked gait, his huge eyes fixed on Dod as if striving to convey to him some message that was beyond words. There was a noise of broken glass and Captain Redstone was on his feet. His mouth was agape, his ancient frame racked through and through with a storm of fury so terrible that it paralysed him and robbed him of speech; he was ghastly, pitiable, holding his stick poised above the little monster crouched at his feet, powerless to bring it down. Kell was pale with emotion, rapturous. Little by little the din in the tavern underwent a change. A woman's sharp laugh rang out. Already two waiters were standing by to intervene. Now Redstone was uttering inarticulate cries and beginning to totter dangerously on his pins. The dwarf was hurling distracted glances around him, imploring assistance which he well knew no one was willing to provide. Suddenly he made a dash for the little door at the back. Dod was through it at his heels.

Out on the alley's gleaming paving-stones he paused for several seconds, motionless, inhaling deeply the misty air of that October night, his ears alert to the dwindling echo. Then, reckoning the creature was far enough ahead, he set off with brisk determination in pursuit.

Dod has been left in the sun, forgotten. He is very hot.
Sweat is pouring down his face. Oozing inexhaustibly
from the pores just below his hairline, it collects in thin,
insinuating rivulets which run down into his eyes, his
mouth, hang on the wings of his nose, drip down inside
his collar. All of summer's fire is already alight in
this May sun as it sits there blazing half-way up the
sky, and Dod, with a pathetic gesture of the hands, tries
every now and then to protect himself from it. He turns
away to escape its cruel dazzle but then his gaze only
scans the deserted park, entreating the solitude,
appealing to those who have left him there. Kell will
certainly be bringing them back in the car. It will be
nothing. And how willingly he will forgive him...
For if he bears him any ill-will it is only half-heartedly.
The fact that the girls should have left him there without further ado and gone off at the first sign from Kell
he is sensible enough to accept as the inflexible operation
of a natural law, whatever the inconvenience to himself.
Dod does not think of questioning the physics of this
world. Girls migrate towards Kell because Kell hollows
out in space, through none of his own doing, a kind of
crater into which they are irresistibly drawn. So he
cannot be angry with Isabelle and Jamyne, can't even
find it in his heart to reproach them, and it would
never so much as occur to him to accuse his little
darlings of behaving off-handedly towards him - how
could it? Bound by the dark fatality of their bodies,
subject at each moment to such a multitude of con-

flicting drives, they are never so distant but that a
fresh impulse will restore almost immediately their
affectionate complaisance. They are very fond of him,
oh sweet conviction, and it was so kind of them to come
and fetch him on this Saturday morning, almost an hour
ago now, in his dingy room. In they burst, burgeoning
flesh barely restrained by their flimsy dresses, their
mouths full of laughter, their hair in disorder, in
they burst, voluble and impatient - ah, he too must
taste the honey of this magnificent May sun! How
tender the companionship of girls! How disturbing
their scent in the first warmth of summer! Dod, out
on the paths of the park, could smell it still, wafted
erratically on the lazy breeze, and from time to time,
turning his head as far round as he could, he tried to
catch a whiff of it off the bare, half-flexed arm that
was pushing his chair. Then Kell arrived. His noisy
little red car pulled up at the edge of the park. From
there in the road, not even bothering to come over to
them, he waved and called and off they ran, Isabelle
and Jamyne...Kell threw an arm round each one and
the three of them remained like that for a moment,
heads together. The girls glanced back at Dod and then
Kell let go of them, walked off a little way, started
gesturing with his hands - Dod is familiar with Kell's
fine, expressive hands - then leaned against the side
of his car, folded his arms, cocked his head on one side
and looked at them with a smile. Isabelle ran over to
Dod and very quickly and breathlessly told him that
they would be back in a few minutes, a quarter of an
hour perhaps, and not to be too impatient. She made
a movement as if to go but immediately checked herself. She appeared to want to say something more and
paused with her mouth open, but finally she said nothing
and her gaze, which had been resting on Dod, detached
itself imperceptibly from him, though without her eyes
moving, and plunged into emptiness, and all of a sudden
the rustling of the leaves became strangely distinct, as

Unexpectedly the alley came out into the Rue des
Bateleurs. Dod was puzzled to find himself in familiar
surroundings after emerging from a thoroughfare whose
name he did not know and which he could not remember
ever having noticed before. Confident though he was in
his star, and half-drunk into the bargain, he doubted
whether the alley had been placed there uniquely for
his benefit, to be used for the headlong pursuit of
deformed creatures or for spying on secret meetings
that very likely had nothing to do with him. Tomorrow
or some other day he would probably come across the
alley again in daylight and it would be shabby-looking
and hold no further mystery. Unless it only existed at
night...He shrugged. But he was in a mood to enjoy
the vagaries of his imagination and he contented himself with adding to the pleasures it gave him by parrying
its thrusts with what he believed to be a critical frame
of mind. He told himself that he was now completely
sober. And he nodded his head to convince himself.
It was a pity, he further reflected with massive sagacity,
that it was foggy, because of course that blurred his
vision. With his feet glued to the pavement and his gaze
a blank, he let the upper part of his body respond to
every gust of the night air.

To the right, in the direction of the Quai des Cygnes,
there was a certain amount of noise and movement. To
the left all was emptiness and silence. Dod caught a
glimpse of the dwarf's silhouette as it crossed the road
and darted into the Rue de Brammone. That snapped

him out of his daze. In fact it cost him a considerable effort to master his first impulse which had been to go tearing after the creature and catch it up. Even so it was not long before he saw it again, standing motionless beneath a street-lamp twenty or thirty paces ahead of him as if it not only knew it was being followed and was making no attempt to get away but was on the contrary so complaisant a quarry as to go out of its way to help the hunter not to lose the scent. The idea flashed through Dod's mind that actually he himself was the prey who was being thus so weirdly lured.

In the cone of smoky light which the street-lamp cut with such geometrical precision through the fog, the dwarf looked like some large insect, trapped by a malevolent hand under a glass funnel. Then, abruptly, Dod saw the trap was sprung. Simultaneously he became aware of the sound of tiny, rapid foot-steps making off in the direction of the Bourdiguen.

A little farther on another street-lamp picked up for the space of a second the twisted black silhouette. And Dod, with joy in his heart and with great mad shouts of laughter that sounded like sobs, addressed as follows this creature who kept systematically giving him the slip:

'Monster...don't try and be too clever. You seem to think...it's you...who's calling the tune. Get this... crazy idea...out of your rudimentary...or primitive... brain, I beg you. No more than our vassal, the lovely Amalia, your accomplice...so expert in innuendo and strong drink... Psst.... Monster, where are you? I... I can see you...I've seen you. I spot you at each of your quantic bursts. Listen to me...I hold all the strings...especially the one I've tied to your crooked leg. I'll...have you by the tail...show you to the Gentlemen...they'll say.... Fine catch. Go and see Agénor the taxidermist, tell him you come from us. Monster... You'll discover to your cost that I know the words and formulae that bind the spirits of earth,

air, fire and water... Etc.... I was a studious youth...
make no mistake...I didn't waste my time. But it's
all dark like a gap in memory. Monster of mischief....
It's obvious, you're just a spirit of the earth, one of
the ancient Serpent's clutch...hatched out by Captain
Redstone.... Peek-a-boo...seen you.... Captain
Redstone was the best incubator of his day. It's a well-
known fact. Nowadays...all he can do...is flap his
scrawny wings...the old goose...whenever his rheumy
eye lights on one of his creatures. But what a grasp he
had! I'm his.... He.... Captain Redstone begot me in
Hampshire.... Me too.... I was nine when I was born.
My mother inhaled some sulphurous fumes escaping
from his laboratory.... She choked...then she saw me.
like being stabbed in the heart. Monster...little maniki
little clock-work...someone gave your spring one hell
of a good wind. But however far you lure me...with
all she made us drink, that servant of ours...it'll be a
long time before I start feeling cold in this October fog
in which we're wrapped and which could easily be
nuptial...or something of the sort, nappy or shroud I
mean.... Everything that's lost in it turns up elsewhere
at number nought, Rue des Blancs-Manteaux...I suppose
madame. But where are you leading me, o intermittent
monster..in the long run?'

The waters of the Bourdiguen were visible at the
end of the street and Dod saw the dwarf make a left
turn on the quay towards the Pont de la Couronne.

A little hurrying figure. Smaller than that of a grown-up, even seen from this distance. A little dark figure hurrying along one of the side-paths. Dod blinks the sweat from his eyes and can then make out a head as big as the rest of the body and limbs so short they can only be withered. The figure is approaching with a jolting, uneven gait in fits and starts, rolling about with sudden little lurches, drawing nearer all the time, soon passing within a few yards of Dod, turning towards him a pair of enormous eyes, catching his gaze and holding it, still holding it even as the creature moves off along a relentless parallel, and now its manner of movement as well as the erratic trotting action of the rudimentary legs is even more reminiscent of some insect struggling home with a prize which is too heavy for it, this bulky black-leather satchel, for example, which Dod has only just noticed and the weight of which hurls its owner from one side of the path to the other and back in such a way that he seems to be more clinging to it and struggling to keep it under control than actually carrying it - and if it's his balance he's worried about, wouldn't he do better to look in front of him with this unbearably empty gaze staring into a chimerical void?

A little dark silhouette hurrying away. But now other creatures have come into view at the edge of the park, turning down the path towards him. Three creatures marching abreast and holding hands. The tallest one is the schoolgirl - Dod recognized her as soon as he saw her. He observes that the dwarf slows his pace the closer he gets to the children, and soon he stops altogether, putting the black satchel down at his feet and waiting. He turns round two or three times and glances in Dod's direction as if hoping for help or looking for a line of retreat. Their tiny steps bring the children inexorably nearer. The dwarf bends down and grasps his satchel, but immediately drops it again. What's the use, he's probably saying to himself. It's very hot and I'm very tired. He pulls out a handkerchief from his pocket and mops his brow. The children, very near him now, take up the whole width of the path.

The group is frozen for a moment in the violent mid-day glare. Then Dod sees the dwarf waving his ridi-culously short arms about and the sound of a high-pitched voice is coming louder now and is accompanied by excited cries from the children. The dwarf suddenly wrenches himself free from the clutches of their tiny hands, staggers backwards with the satchel clasped to his chest, loses his balance, falls over and stays there, sitting on the ground in the middle of the path, while the schoolgirl grasps her little brothers by the hand and all three of them make off at a run, pursued by the voice uttering more and more strident cries.

When the children are level with Dod they cut across the lawn towards him. Back where they have come from a little, dark silhouette is hurrying off and disappears round a bend in the path.

'You saw,' says the schoolgirl, 'how wicked he is.' And lowering her voice she adds, 'He's got gold in his satchel.'

She turns to the boys and snaps out, 'Say hello.' Then examines Dod, observes his flushed face, the sweat on his forehead, his hair damp and awry: 'Why do you stay in the sun?'

'Someone's coming to fetch me in a moment...' And Dod attempts a confident smile.

The two boys are staring at him with embarrassing curiosity. 'Doesn't he walk at all?' asks the taller one.

'He's an invalid,' explains the schoolgirl. 'His legs have died.' She takes her brother's hand and places it on Dod's calf. 'Feel. See? - it's dead.'

He feels it cautiously and then whips his hand away and plunges it in his pocket.

'Invalids have to be helped,' says the schoolgirl. And she passes out of sight behind Dod's chair.

Dod is wheeled through unknown territory to the most remote corner of the park. Turning his head to right and left he can see the two boys marching stiffly along slightly behind him, their eyes fixed on a point in the distance, their faces set in expressions of almost military gravity. They have each placed one hand on the chair in order to participate symbolically in its progress. Directly behind him is the invisible schoolgirl; Dod is aware of her breathing, accentuated as it is by exertion.

'Shouldn't we go back now?' he says without hope. 'I'm afraid your parents will be worried about you not coming home.'

This is not considered worthy of a reply.

At the eastern edge of the park are some clumps of woodland left over from the old du Theil estate. There among the trees, in the middle of a lawn surrounded by a fence of wire netting, is preserved - out of respect for the past? - one of those insipid products of a decadent age of sculpture such as are found to this day in public gardens and in the few large estates that survive in this century. It is meant to represent some languid-bodied Adonis but the pose, with the head thrown back against the right shoulder and one hand raised to eye-level as if to ward off some threat - the intentions of the artist are far from clear, especially since the ephebe's face is rendered totally without expression - is oddly suggestive of an attitude of ear and defensiveness. Dod is pushed right up against the fence and it remains only for him to wonder what is expected of him. A glance

155

reveals that the children are still paying no attention to him. On the contrary, they appear to be captivated by this piece of statuary; the two boys are staring at it with dazzled faces, looking directly into the sun, their features puckered in two identical grimaces. Dod says to himself that they are obviously trying to put him in the way of some artistic emotion, but despite his good will and his desire to be pleasant to the children his eyes hurt too much and he simply does not feel up to a sufficiently protracted contemplation to receive the touch of grace. So he lets his gaze wander over his surroundings and discovers three large dogs - mongrels, but corresponding in size and build to the type generally referred to as wolf-hounds. They are snuffling around in the grass, separated by several yards from one another and appearing, in a surly and disillusioned manner, to be following some scent. One of the dogs sneezes and the others look up. All three turn towards Dod, consider him for a moment with expressions of bored disgust, then move off unhurriedly among the trees and are soon lost to view. A cloud passes over the sun and the glaring light is abruptly dimmed. It now being a less painful matter to look at the statue, Dod subjects it to a listless examination. He is astonished to find its expressionless mask gradually becoming more and more familiar, and all of a sudden understands the reason why he has been brought here - and is simultaneously unwilling to admit it - for he has recognized his own face.

When Dod recovered his senses the children had gone.

Little lazy moons clustered around the baroque lamp-standards on the Pont de la Couronne. The drifting curtains of fog parted lazily here and there over the Bourdiguen to reveal the black water streaked with restless glints of gold. It was a desolate, soundless pageant, a stately carnival staged by the night for her own amusement.

The creature was almost at the middle of the bridge when Dod thought he saw it turn round. At the same instant he lost sight of it. The bridge, after spanning the waters of the Bourdiguen, continued beyond a narrow strip of land across the Bardo Canal which here ran parallel. Before Dod was a third of the way across he saw Mme Arthème's ghost emerge from the fog, rippling towards him along the top of the right-hand parapet. Gesturing profusely, he upbraided it as follows:

'Madame go home to bed. You're too old to be running about at night. Go on, go home.... You're superfluous now. What the devil - can't you see things have changed? What the devil.... The devil's social utility, madame, has now been acknowledged. Really. He's invited to baptisms, communions and festivals of commemoration. People lay poppies on graves. You give them to the woman you love. Love itself has become magical. Lovers change shape between each embrace. It's most amusing. And the possibilities of harmonious conjunction are endless. Discussions are organized at which young girls analyze their erotic experiences. Intellectuals attend in force. The theatre is no longer as you knew it.

157

Actors flash across the stage with dizzying speed, a
single one sufficing for twenty roles. One or two even
contrive to play the audience. At the end of the performance actors, audience and stage staff experience
such ecstasies that they merge into one incandescent
mass. The curtains catch fire and the survivors rush
screaming into the streets. So infectious is their joy
that immediately a wave of suicides spreads through
the town. The traffic police drop dead at their posts
from shock. People come from miles around to admire
the expressions of ineffable bliss which their faces
preserve in death. You can see for yourself this is no
world for you. So be off with you, flee, fond guardian
of my memories, flee, sweet chair-attendant.... Go
on, beat it, you old fool.... Before hell finds out
you're here. '

Laughing, sobbing and waving his arms, Dod drove
the elusive shape of Mme Arthème before him, now
along one parapet, now along the other. Suddenly it
was gone: the fog had reclaimed what it had so capriciou
yielded up. But Dod had not time to savour his triumph.
Remembering the dwarf, he set off again at a run.

On the far side of the canal the bridge gave onto a
little square whose name he had never known. In the
centre of it was a miniature version of the Great
Sphinx. Every little abrasion of time and the desert
sand had been reproduced with the minutest attention
to detail without the figure losing any of the chilly gloss
of irremediable modernity. The fog at least granted it
a measure of suggestiveness. But Dod, not even
deigning to give it a glance, ran on straight ahead. A
few yards from the fork between the Rue de la Dame-
au-Lys and the Rue Jeanne he came to a puzzled halt.
His glance, erring from one street to the other, found
nothing to indicate which he should take. Then he heard
hurrying foot-steps and soon saw, coming towards him
down the Rue de la Dame-au-Lys, the figure of a man
wearing a hat and hunched in an overcoat. Possibly for

fear of meeting anyone who might distract him from the affair in hand, he instinctively took the Rue Jeanne.

The dwarf loomed up out of the fog less than a hundred yards ahead. Dod flung himself into an open doorway. Yet he saw no sign that his presence had been discovered, although the noise of his pursuit must have been clearly audible. The dwarf went on jogging along, no longer hurrying now but moving with a dismayingly calm assurance. As if he had crossed some boundary and were now on familiar territory.

And so they went on, one behind the other, a hundred yards apart, the code now know, the conventions implicitly accepted. Down the deserted streets of the colonial quarter where not one voice or strain of lingering music betrayed the slightest sign of life, where not a single light shone in the barred and narrow windows. But the fog, as they left the canal and the sea behind them and climbed towards the upper part of the town, became progressively thinner.

At one point the dwarf deviated from his hitherto unswerving course and, whether by whim or design, took a turning as if he were heading for the Place Radegonde. But at the first cross-roads he turned north again towards Les Affanies Park the sombre foliage of which came into view a few minutes later at the end of the street. And Dod spoke to the creature: 'Like a fish...you have hooked on the end of your line. Drawing me, drawing me...towards what shore? Or down...down to what muddy bed? Look, I'm no trouble. Patient, submissive.... A perfect dear of a docile little fish who asks for no more than to eat from your hand. Does that leave you unmoved, you monster of indifference? ...But watch out - I could climb up the line to the fisherman. I have eyes to see him, hands to seize him.... Queer fish indeed. Or perhaps... just a piece of muck stuck to your shoe, soon to be scraped off on the kerb? H'm.... Too humble, I agree. But I tell you.... Never mind what I tell you. I love

you...you lovable monster. I would follow you on
bended knee.... I would.... Ah! my heart is too heavy
to bear.... I can't go through with it. Do I want to go
through with it? To the end? To what end...old
Bucephalus.... False charger.... Monster of Perfidy..
Fathomless night.... To think I so cleverly took all
the short-cuts up to now so as to stay close...to our
little revels. Crafty Dod.... Sitting securely on the
fence, having his cake and scoffing it too. That couldn't
last.... That could.... That that that that that! And
now.... Fish! Where are you...soft lights? Sparkling
laughter of our girls.... Getting pleasantly drunk....
The gay life.... Gone! Of course...I had to end up
looking a fool...in this greedy night...which will never
return any of what one gives it.... Escape? Perhaps
there's still time.... There's no time... It's...what
time? Monster...what's the time? But the monster
surely has no watch.... He is governed by tropisms....
like the little flowers are. A tropic monster, yes
sir.... I'm afraid. Yes sir. I'm afraid. Yes sir, I
confess.... I'm afraid. I'd adapted too well to a
desire that had become harmless for having lost its
object. Yes sir, yes sir, I digress, quite true, I'm
dark, darkness, no I'm no more, I am , even so, dark,
yes, dark the way others are negro, it's in the genes,
nothing you can do, only give a doleful smile. This
desire, then.... I'm too absent-minded, I forget even
elementary things. Like...for example...when you
summon the devil you shouldn't step out of the circle....
My good old circle! The most comfortable circle that
ever.... I would have lived my life.... Old age would
have come.... Forgetfulness.... Peace.... The
reassuring feeling of a duty left undone.... Because
there was no duty to do. And then...to look back, and
smile, and say...oh God...blessed be that happy mis-
fortune. And then to step out into the summer night
among the dancing fire-flies.... So I fail to see why I
persist in following you...idiot that I am. And how

shall hope be endured when it threatens one with certainty?'

As Dod entered through the park gates a cold silence fell in his heart.

Dod and Dr. Nauser are sitting face to face by the
window, smiling at one another, Dod in his wheel-chair,
Dr. Nauser straddling his chair and resting his folded
arms on the back of it, a posture which gives him a
somewhat rounded back and makes his neck disappear
into his shoulders; his long face, thrust forward in this
way from the rest of his body, achieves an expression
which is at once attentive and good-natured. From
time to time one or other of them casts a careless
glance in the direction of Adrienne's window, a move
which his opposite number spots immediately but
considers too unimportant to pass the slightest remark
about it, even in jest. It is a very mild summer evening
of the kind that favours the dreamy stroll, relaxed
conversation and a feeling of quiet contentment at being
alive.

'It's getting near the holidays, ' says Dr. Nauser.
'You surely won't be spending the whole summer at
Sarmes, will you?'

Dod shrugs as if to say: Be it according to the will
of heaven. The doctor indicates with an expansive
gesture the landscape stretching away before them.

'There's a place for you in this world, ' he says.
'There's no such thing as wasted time. '

'It seems to me, ' says Dod quietly, 'that my place
is where I am, here, is it not?'

'You've a wicked wit, you little blighter.... Ah,
well, let's say you've been saved in spite of yourself,
if it makes you feel any better - I don't begrudge you

162

that little pleasure. We call it...Grace.'

'Of which you are the bounteous dispenser.... But now that I'm saved what am I going to do?'

'Live, lad. Live. And that's more than enough. Let's see you lift that little leg again.'

Dod very slowly raises his right leg and even more slowly lowers it down beside the left one. Dr. Nauser gives a nod.

'Isn't that wonderful? Soon you'll be moving the other one. How pleased your mum and dad are going to be; I'll drop them a line this evening as ever is. I've no doubt at all they'll jump on the first train to come and admire the miracle. Yes, my boy, yes.... At last you'll be able to make reasonable use of your lower limbs. The world is full of excellent paths all leading back to where you started from. No danger of getting lost.'

'If you come back to where you started from, what's the point?'

'Exactly the kind of remark one might expect from the little idiot you seem to like to be taken for. But you can't fool me. And you know very well, in spite of yourself, that what I'm doing is what you in your heart of hearts really want. You're cut out for happiness.'

'Of what kind?'

'The kind that comes from following this precept of the Mishnah: Fix not your gaze on what is above, nor on what is below, nor before, nor behind. And it is further said: whoever dare transgress this rule, it were better for him that he had never been born.'

'An excellent principle indeed. Have you others to recommend me?'

'Be satisfied with this. It embraces all others.'

'I feel I am going to be happy.'

Dr. Nauser's beaming face suddenly becomes stern and grim; at the same time his gaze darkens with an emotion not unlike pity.

'It is your duty to be so. After a modest fashion.

163

A human fashion. And I don't like that bitterness
behind your words. You've inhaled too many poisoned
vapours and I can understand that they have left their
mark on you. But since we're on the subject of the
Scriptures, you inveterate reader, do you remember
the four famous doctors who entered the Garden...and
who were in a better position than yourself to meet all
the perils that beset the mind in want of understanding.
For these were four excellent doctors, four powerful
minds, refined by study and radiant with all the light
of intelligence and faith. They entered the Garden, and
Ben Azai died, Ben Zoma went mad, Elia ben Abuya
lost his faith....'

'But the fourth, Akiba, came back safe and sound,
and had acquired Knowledge.'

'I have good reason to believe that he was the un-
luckiest of all and that he lived on under the false
colours of a fraudulent knowledge. Believing he had
culled the living truth, he failed to see that he held a
withered branch. And none of it would have happened
had the watchman been at his post or had he not allowed
his vigilance to slumber. For there was a watchman.'

'I am more fortunate. The watchman has come out
to meet me.'

Dr. Nauser cocks his head on one side and says with
a wink, 'The thing I like about you, my young friend, is
your sense of humour. That's why I'm so fond of you.'

Then he turns towards Mme Luffergal as she comes
out of the kitchen wheeling the table on which she has
laid out Dod's supper.

'And you, Mme Luffergal,' he says, 'I'm very fond
of you too.'

Pine, cypress, spruce and yew formed the sombre,
unvarying vegetation of Les Affanies Park. The dwarf
pursued a tortuous course down one path after another
and in the shadowy gloom cast by the trees, despite
the fact that at this altitude the fog was virtually non-
existent - a few stars twinkled between the branches
overhead - not only had Dod soon lost his sense of
direction but also, for all his following the creature
so dangerously close, almost treading on its heels as
it were, he suddenly found himself alone. He was in
the middle of a round open space where several paths
converged. The sound of foot steps was still faintly
audible but Dod, unable to decide their course, plunged
panic-stricken down the path which lay straight ahead
of him, half out of his mind at the idea that he might
never emerge from the chilly obscurity of the garden.
He did, however, very quickly emerge from it and
to his great surprise found himself standing outside
the gates, both reassured and at the same time
mysteriously disappointed, in a street where graceful
street-lamps cast their limpid light on a row of
bourgeois façades belonging to one of the residential
quarters of the upper town. Not far off, strolling
calmly along the kerb, was the dwarf, his coat-collar
turned up and his hands thrust into his pockets. Could
the game then go on beyond the sepulchral garden and
its labyrinthine paths where fear stalked abroad? Dod
laughed indulgently at himself and at the volatility of
his emotions. He told himself it was getting late and

agreed with himself that at least he had had a walk
which could without exaggeration be described as
stimulating, but let's leave something for the future,
he concluded - oh wisdom, etc. Just as he was admirin
these resolves and even more the young man responsibl
for their formulation he saw the dwarf dart into a narro
side-street or alley that showed as a dark gash between
the fine façades of aple stone; a bollard at the entrance,
barring entry to vehicles, indicated that it was a private
footpath. He said to himself he would perhaps just take
a look.

The alley was empty. But a few yards down a
rectabgle of light fell across the pavement. Dod came
to a halt before a door that stood wide open on a lighted
hall; at the far end of the hall a spiral stair case climbe
through its own shadow to the lighted zone of the first
floor.

'I was the plaything of a shadow,' Olivier is saying. 'Of course, I look pretty stupid, I know that, no need to tell me. But you don't give a damn. Nor do I. You can't imagine how little I care. About looking stupid. About all this.... Tomorrow I'm off to Rome. Rome, Florence, Venice.... Art. Beauty. See? ...Far from these little accidents our sensibility is heir to. We're meeting again in London at the end of September. We've agreed not to see each other till then. We're being sensible, you see. Let time tell. Time.... You're doing that too, aren't you - letting time tell? No, you don't give a damn about time. But eternity.... The Absolute. The Absolute, isn't that right? I have a feeling I'll be joining you before long. Then there'll be two of us to gaze upon the monotonous flux of phenomena. Doesn't that give you a kick?'

Dod glances up at him absent-mindedly and returns to his musing.

As Dod set foot on the first-floor landing the light went
out. Several seconds later his hand, groping round the
door-frame, came upon something which might have
been the button of a bell. He pressed it gingerly,
wondering whom or what he was about to alert by this
simple gesture. It was only when the light came on
again that he realized he had been as scared as a little
child in the dark.

Two double-doors faced each other across the landing
The one nearest him bore a white-metal plaque engraved
with the letters TAU and nothing else. He was still
hesitating when he heard footsteps and the sound of
voices coming from above. Then someone was rapidly
descending the stairs. Afraid to be seen standing there
a stranger bent on some equivocal purpose - Dod hurried
on up, passing after a few steps a youth in a black
sweater who took no notice of him. He had automatically
continued climbing and was now on the second-floor
landing. Below, above and all around him - silence.
TAU.... The three mysterious letters resolved themselves into a single Greek consonant as myriad
associations began to form in the mind of this impenitent
devourer of abstruse literature - Dod, of course -
hermetic symbols, ageless cults, arcana, gnoses,
mystical tenebrae...which the time-switch promptly
turned into actual tenebrae. But not before he had
noticed that one of the two doors on that floor stood
ajar, and now he observed - and forgot on the instant
his intention of returning downstairs - a throbbing of

lights in the gap between door and jamb, as if an
illuminated sign had been shining through a window into
the dark interior. He pushed open the door.

He found himself in what might have been a studio -
a photographer's? - a fairly large room lined through-
out on walls and ceiling with black paper. A small
screen in the middle focussed the only light and colour
and movement in the room in the form of sumptuous
kaleidoscopic images which altered with a kind of
vegetal slowness. Lying on mats facing the screen
were a number of people, young people, four or five
of them, some with their heads raised on folded arms,
others leaning on one elbow, recumbant figures, only
their avid eyes negating the immobility of the tomb....

...And the eyes shone and the faces changed in the
changing light, now tinged with the glow of fugitive
dawns, now suddenly livid masks of the drowned plunging
dreamily into the depths of some submarine cavern....

Embarrassed, ill at ease and vaguely ashamed, as
if he had interrupted some strange intimacy, Dod let
his gaze slide over the motionless bodies and concentrated all his attention on the screen. After several
minutes, disappointed at experiencing nothing to resemble
the ecstasy he had seen reflected in those defenceless
faces, he looked away, and then he began to make out
what looked like graffiti chalked up here and there on
the walls, but without being able to decipher them in
the darkness, except for a few words on one line at eye-
level; these he read as it were letter by letter during
brighter periods in the projection, not even needing to
read to the end, reconstituting the rest of the inscription
in his mind: Qui non est in lumine illumine me.

Hacked crudely in the stone.... Olivier had been
there too. They had deciphered it together in a dark
corner of the ruined chapel. Those walks in the forest,
their truancies which next day became adventures....
And the exhileration with which they had bandied
opinions about that mysterious invocation in a dialect

which did not belong to their part of the country but came, they were convinced, from some enchanted land, and which he was so surprised to come across again here, amid what appeared to be the most sophisticated manifestations of the modern spirit - and so far from the superstitious rural environment in which he had grown up, and from the terrifying stories told him by his aged cousins of whom there were sometimes two and sometimes three. Then a hand was laid lightly on his arm.

Through a door which, because it was also covered with black paper, he had not noticed before, he was shown into a small room lit feebly by a low table-lamp. This made him blink as if it had been a flood-light after the semi-darkness of the studio.

The woman standing beside him was severely beautiful. Clad entirely in black, she presented a figure that was so to speak abstract - deliberately so. Her purity of form, her serious expression, everything about her betrayed her determination to let nothing appear that might seduce the imagination, even less appeal to the senses. Yet Dod felt that she was kindly disposed towards him, and it even seemed to him that there was tenderness and sympathy in her look as she asked him: 'Do you like these light-shows?'

Her voice was low-pitched, slightly husky, and yet... somehow faintly tremulous, as if with a residue of suppressed laughter. Dod was disturbed and immediately on the alert, anxious, suspicious and tempted to make his escape, but she took his hand and made him sit down beside her on a divan. She then proceeded to take such a judicious and discreet interest in him and showed herself to be so kind and understanding that he believed he had found in her that elder sister whom everyone, sooner or later, finds he needs. All fear and mistrust dispelled, he laid his soul naked before her.

At one point she stood up and he thought sadly that she was already going, but it was only to say, 'It

170

would be a pity if these light-shows gave you no pleasure at all....'

And seeing her smile he was happy again and filled with agreeable thoughts. Then she was once more sitting beside him. Never, he said to himself, had any creature made him feel so deeply secure. With a kindly gesture she offered him a glass which was half-full of a slightly cloudy, perhaps opalescent liquid. It tasted of nothing in particular and it was only vaguely that he became aware, two or three minutes later, of a faint bitterness lingering on his lips. At that very instant an adorable creature leaned towards him.

...Her eyes were shining, her lips slightly parted, and all of a sudden she was miraculously near and looking at him so warmly and tenderly that he felt almost faint with a kind of voluptuous dizziness. The face which before had been ideally beautiful was now flushed with colour, the crimson mouth had a swollen look, the austere dress was now stretched taut over a trembling body whose slightest movement drew flashes of fire from some invisible furnace....

But they were on their feet now and she was holding him by the hand. She led him back into the studio and helped him recline on one of the vacant mats. He gave a sigh of pleasure, feeling very much better now that he was lying down. The mere effort of trying to prop himself up one elbow was enough to bring back the giddiness that had made him almost fall in getting up from the divan. Luckily she had supported him; that had been kind of her. He wanted to thank her...but she was already gone. The intensified glare of the screen took possession of his mind.

Oh, come back, come back.... How he.... A tremendous pressure is forcing him flat against the floor.... Through it.... He is plummeting downwards.... Call her! One look from her compassionate eyes and he would be saved.... She'd have the power to retrieve

him...from this world in liquefaction.... Just one
look.... A wave like a whole ocean swamps him....

Dod, waking up in the middle of the night, discovers
he is wet. Confusion worse confounded.... Then sudden
fear. Has it come to this? Has his body's frailty
chosen this way to throw him well and truly back to
early infancy? He tells himself he ought to change his
pyjamas. The cupboard containing his clean linen is
within easy reach. But he shrinks from the effort
such an operation would require, retreating, as usual,
under cover of his tiredness. What would be the good
of clean pyjamas when the sheets are wet? When Mme
Luffergal comes to make his bed she can hardly ignore
the tell-tale signs of nocturnal incontinence. This
thought calms him. Mme Luffergal will change the
sheets without comment. It is even likely that she will
form no opinion of her own on the subject. One need
expect from her neither surprise nor disapproval, nor
any more interest in this than she would show in a
spider's web or a slug on a lettuce leaf she happened
to be rinsing. Her inscrutability is total. A foreign
power, utterly beyond compromise. Her vast presence
fills the little room no more than the wind does space.
Dod derives comfort from existing so little in her eyes.
He relaxes with a sigh. Blissful images take shape in
his mind. The dampness in which he is lying, far from
bothering him, brings him a feeling of peace such as
he can never remember experiencing before. Smiling
at his innocence, he goes back to sleep.

Cold. Icy ocean waves. Adrift.... Sliding endlessly
down slopes yet remaining forever at the same spot,
the same level.... Or is it that here and elsewhere have
become once and for all the same - have merged? A
feeling then that one could get used to it. Followed by
a feeling that it has always been so. No, not always....
Memory of a time when one lived in the presence of
Her. Her look. Then again oblivion. The water's
cold caress.... A shedding of one's form, leaving it
to the mercy of the waves. A dissolution. Sweetness...
An immense sweetness.... Caress of warm water...
as sweet as the touch of Her hand. A mist floating
above the ocean. Being also that mist. Balmy.
Sweetness. Balm. Being now an incarnation of the
substance of dreams...of vague, unsettled functions,
innumerable because all mingling in one another...
useless, because having no body to serve. Dreaming
of being a dream of.... And all...with the most
exquisite lack of precision. Sweetness. A sound....
Memory of the age-old song of the blood coursing in
the veins? To what purpose? The waters of this
ocean are thicker than blood, richer than blood,
warmer.... A whole ocean evaporating away. That
sound.... That terrifying sound.... The waters
parting.... The beam picking out his knee.... The
glare of dazzlement.... Pain.... Dazzlement....
Dizziness....

Dod sees the light go on. Then he hears someone
very slowly and carefully closing the door. Tiny,
shuffling footsteps start to nibble at the silence. He
knows already who is coming. He tries to hold his
breath the better to follow the footsteps' minute, interminable advance. But he begins to suffocate. Oh
terror, terror - world of teeth and claws. Dod flees
to the deepest part of the cave. When his mother
finally appears she looks tiny and black as if standing
at the end of a tunnel. Keeping his voice low, he asks:
'Is that you, mum?'

She comes a little closer, she steps inside the alcove,
and then the smooth, yellow familiar face is smiling
down at him.

'I didn't want to wake you, my child,' she says.
And sighs. 'Your father's asleep. Of course, he loves
you too in his way. But he has other things on his mind.
He's preoccupied with himself. But I couldn't sleep a
wink for thinking about you all the while. What a disappointment.... After Dr. Nauser's letter we were
quite expecting to find you practically standing up and
walking again.... We know Dr. Nauser. But for the
last few days you haven't even got out of bed.... What
are we to make of that? And the doctor's away.... So
I got up and dressed without making a sound. When you
used to be ill I got up every night to come and sit by
your bed. Your father went on sleeping. He's always
done his duty by you and there's nothing can be said
against him on that score. He's worked hard all his

life. But all men are the same - he couldn't stand hearing you cry at night....'

'He'll be worried if he wakes up and finds you not there,' murmurs Dod.

'He won't wake up,' she says, and her gentle smile returns. 'After supper I gave him his sleeping draught, as I do every evening. I gave him a little bit extra this time.'

Dod feels the clamminess of the damp linen against his thighs and gives a sudden shiver. He believes he can detect a faint ammoniacal smell. He carefully pulls the sheet up around him but the smell persists. He takes a few little soundless sniffs so as to get a better idea of its strength and penetration. His mother's smile has disappeared. He anxiously studies her face for the first sign of that pinched look which will tell him that she is aware of his incontinence.

'You were my consolation,' she is saying. 'We were so happy, do you remember? Oh, the blessed days we had. Your father used to go off every morning and we'd be left alone, just the two of us. I used to do your hair like a little girl's. You told me that when you grew up you'd ask me to marry you. We had our little secrets together.'

Her head is wobbling a little above her stiffly held body with a very slight up-and-down movement like a leaf in an imperceptible breeze. Her eyes are half-shut and she looks so absorbed that for a moment Dod is seized with a ridiculous fear that this head is going to topple off and come crashing down on him like a boulder. And his thoughts begin to wander.... At nights, all night, perhaps every night, mum's head will be there, sitting on my chest, and I'll not be able to breathe, with mum's heavy head on my chest, right in front of my eyes, and I'll hear her speak, and she'll scold me because I've done wee-wees in the bed....
He tries to recapture the smell of which he has ceased to become aware, lifting the sheet a little.

She has been rummaging around in her ancient black-leather bag and now brings out an incongruously shiny-looking plastic wallet. She polishes it on her sleeve, opens it, searches for a moment and finds a photograph. Dod stares gloomily at a picture of himself.

'Remember?' she asks, smiling. 'It was taken just before you left us.'

Her words are loaded with incomprehensible innuendo and she holds the photograph in front of her son's face longer than necessary. He puts out a hand to take it, not in order to examine it more closely - out of complacency or self-indulgence - but because his embarrassment has become so intolerable that he cannot bear the confrontation for so much as a second longer. He feels like a person caught naked looking at himself in a mirror and overwhelmed by a sense of shame as sudden as panic at this twofold violation of his nudity, once by the intruder's eyes and once by his own which have irrevocably surrendered to the other his most intimate image of himself. Dod, his modesty threatened, puts out a hand to take the photograph, but his mother snatches it quickly away with a little laugh and substitutes another portrait, that of a girl wearing a white dress, a very short dress - one can see half-way up her thighs, and since she is leaning forward slightly the neck-line of her dress reveals the cleft between her breasts. Although the photograph is an old one and the colours have faded Dod is uneasily aware of the texture of all this flesh, the more so since it stands out very white and clear against the sombre foliage of a garden.

'Recognize me?' asks his mother. 'I was seventeen then.' And she goes on, 'I look tired, don't I? That's because I was having my period.'

And she smiles with an air of complicity.

The cells of his body are exploding one by one. Myriad tiny explosions. Going pop - or rather po'p. A very gentle sound like fragile membranes bursting. A noise like bubbles.... His whole body is fizzing and bubbling. But he feels nothing. It is all happening to one side. Below. A feeling of being hardly concerned. Hardly even conscious. Rather...just aware. Knowing one is disintegrating. That's all. Innumerable cells exploding infinitesimally one after another. It will be a long process. But probably not as long as one thinks. Until one is reconstituted elsewhere.... More or less.

Dod woke up in a room he did not know. A room that
emerged from a fog of confusing and vaguely painful
sensations, the first incontestable certainty to come
as it were crawling out of the swamp that was his mind -
accompanied by an unpleasant feeling of being wrapped
in stiff garments which had been soaked and then
allowed to dry on him. In fact he was quite naked and
lying in a large warm bed, but the mere touch of the
sheets irritated his skin. He could see his clothes
strewn untidily on an armchair that was upholstered
in wine-coloured rep. There was a taste of bitterness
in his mouth. A sharp pain was nagging at his right
temple and he turned his sore eyes away from the
ridiculous little lamp with its pleated shade that re-
vealed his ugly, depressing surroundings. A hideous
greyish wallpaper lined the walls and the massive rustic
furniture took up an incongruous amount of space in
the small urban interior. He wondered how they had
ever got the enormous wardrobe inside for the top was
practically scraping the ceiling, and he wondered more
particularly why it was so familiar to him, as if it
brought back some childhood memory.

Something, though - was it a smell? - suggested that
the room might well belong to a woman, although he
could see none of the things a woman might ordinarily
be expected to leave lying around. On the contrary,
the dusty furniture and the general air of sadness and
neglect conjured up the image of some seedy bachelor
returning home late at nights and getting up early,

indifferent to the walls that guarded his slumbers - and then Dod said to himself he knew that smell. He thought he could hear the rain drumming on the panes and he was going to get up and open the window and he would see the garden and the white fence and Mrs. Mabel Crocker-Jones beneath her big red umbrella, looking prim and at the same time secretly satisfied as if it were she who had made it rain. But there was nothing here to resemble his pretty little English room, nothing at all, no of course not, how stupid, nothing here suggested Hampshire, least of all that cumbersome wardrobe as stuffed with secrets as the house his aged cousins lived in, or more likely empty, as empty as Amélie's room. . . .

His gaze wandered over the pattern of variously tinted lines on the wallpaper - which was pale blue and not grey as he had thought at first - a whole tangle of lines in which he could not identify a single shape, but still kept on trying, nothing being bearable until it had been given its name, and so finally made out the silhouette of a reaper with lowered scythe, and all around him corn-stocks, and farther off trees, and then he noticed that the fellow was holding his scythe left-handed, which planted a doubt in his mind, and immediately the reaper was replaced by someone standing up in a boat and pushing on a pole, and the stocks and the trees became palaces of some spectral Venice. The gondolier was not entirely satisfactory, but instead of disappearing in his turn in favour of a more convincing figure he suddenly sprouted a beard, adopted the reaper's straw hat and immediately took on such a sarcastic appearance, such an air of improbability, that Dod shut his eyes. . . .

. . . Dozed, perhaps for several minutes, and opened his eyes to find Amalia standing at the foot of the bed. And then he recognized the scent that had intrigued him. They talked.

'You were completely unconscious when I brought

180

you here,' she said. 'Mary Seymour rang me at the Lovely Lady. She didn't know what to do with you.'

'You mean to say that woman was....'

'Whatever did you think, then? Of course it was her. She did have a feeling you hadn't recognized her. It's true she often changes her appearance.... It's because of her job. Still, you should have guessed. After all you'd followed Basal all the way to her place, hadn't you?'

'Basal?'

'The dwarf.' She yawned, smiled apologetically and added, 'It's very late. It'll be light in less than an hour.'

She undressed quickly and got in beside Dod.

Mme Arthème is standing by the bed. She has loomed
up out of the depths of Dod's sleep and is standing there
by his bedside like a tall grey flame that curiously enough
seems to flicker from time to time as if at some colder
blast out of a troubled night. How sad she looks.

'I would have liked to have come earlier,' she says,
the words dying on her lips.

One large pale hand emerges from the front of the
cape, goes up to her face, touches it - inspecting it,
Dod realizes, and he notes with astonishment: She is
ill at ease. He would like to cheer her up, reassure
her - preposterous idea - at least he could invite her
to take a seat. But he cannot remember ever seeing
her sitting down.

'I couldn't come any earlier,' she says.

And then falls silent, like someone surprised by
the echo of their own words murmured in the vast and
almost empty waiting-room of a hospital, and just at
that moment a child screams far off, doors slam,
footsteps hurriedly approach and the fear, so meti-
culously suppressed all one's life, the fear lifts its
little weasel's snout into the anaemic light. And how
one regrets ever having disturbed the silence.

Two minutes have passed, perhaps three. Mme
Arthème is still silent, turning her head this way and
that, searching for the fissure through which to slip
into this space which for the first time ignores her
presence. This evening she does not belong here.
She is a stranger. However desperately she tries to

182

stiffen her bearing, and this stiffness can be sensed
even in the folds of her cape, it seems at each moment
as if she must disappear for good, defeated by so much
hostility. It even seems as if her gaze does not actually
reach things but shrinks back just before touching them,
like the hypersensitive feelers of some way insect. But
as Dod is contemplating this phenomenon - which is all
the more interesting for being, in the case of Mme
Arthème, so totally unexpected - she recovers herself
and utters one final affirmation of her presence.

'I am sorry to have woken you, child, it's very late,
but I have a great deal to do and I'm leaving tomorrow.'

'You're leaving?' asks Dod, trying to put into his
words the surprise and emotion he ought in the normal
way to experience at such an announcement.

Mme Arthème's face brightens and her explanation is
almost voluble: 'I've been hesitating for ages, but the
time I was given to think about it expired today. What
a difficult decision. Finally I've given my agreement.
I went to the post office this morning, even hesitating
again before writing out the telegram. You see why I
haven't mentioned anything to you about it. I didn't
want to tell you before I'd made up my mind. I left it
till the last minute. There are so many things to keep
me here....'

Then, more calmly, resuming her natural manner,
she goes on: 'I have been offered a post as warden of
a children's home in the Alps. It is an interesting job
and a quite unexpected opportunity. I couldn't hope for
another one like it. I'm not as young as I was and if I
may say so I've grown a little weary of this uncertain
existence.'

Dod proceeds to acquaint her with his satisfaction
at seeing due recognition granted at last to the merits
of a person he esteems more than any other in the
world and of his grief at losing, by the same token,
his protectress and irreplaceable friend. She stares
at him long and deliberately.

'My child,' she says, 'I shall never see you again.'

Dod protests. However arduous her duties will she not from time to time have a few free days? Communications are a simple matter in this day and age and the means of travel both convenient and numerous.

'And who knows - later on, once I'm better, I'll be able to come and join you and work by your side. I've several times considered directing my studies more towards teaching. I believe, in fact, I have - am I wrong? - a certain pedagogic gift.'

But her voice is harsh as she says: 'You don't need me any more. Would I leave if you did? I fail to see why I should make any further contribution towards maintaining a lie by continuing to act as your accomplice, although it was against my will and I am, alas, when all's said and done, simply another victim of your duplicity.'

'I fear there must be some misunderstanding,' suggests Dod cautiously in reply, adding, 'I would so love to help you clear it up.'

'You'll be going back to Dr. Nauser. He's re-opened his clinic and I think he can take you at the end of this week. I see no other solution. Staying here with only Mme Luffergal to look after you....'

'She's very devoted.'

'All she can do is prepare the meals you no longer touch, not that that matters to her - she'll go on serving them up and clearing them away just the same until eventually someone tells her to stop. I can see her conscientiously bathing your corpse morning after morning.... As for going back to your parents, certainly not, quite out of the question now, you couldn't stand the journey, and anyway your parents, your poor parents, your poor mother especially, after this dreadful disappointment they're shattered, they're quite incapable of taking care of you - in the state you're in. You're going to Dr. Nauser's. The fact of the matter is he doubts whether he can do any more for

184

you. He's even started having doubts about himself, about Science.... Him - Dr. Nauser! and it's all your doing.'

'One does one's level best to live without being a bother to anyone but even that is too ambitious. How deeply I fell for Dr. Nauser, how sad I am, how I would love him to be happy - and you too, dear Mme Arthème, though you look with such ill-will upon one who has ever entertained with regard to yourself feelings of a quasi-filial nature.'

'It's myself I blame. And my blindness.' Mme Arthème sighs. 'So many wasted years. I really and genuinely tried to lead you into adulthood.'

'I have been too heavy a burden for you.'

'Too light. I was carrying a shadow.'

'Have you found me nothing but a source of disappointment?'

'You slept and I prolonged your sleep. I believed I was doing the right thing. I had at my disposal all the most powerful drugs against dreams. One day, I used to say to myself, he will wake up and come out and quite naturally take his place in the world. You could have lived.'

'Your dispositions were most prudent.'

'But instead, under cover of your immobility, you cultivated every kind of disorder.'

'Isn't that going too far?'

'So many mistakes. And you never failed to take advantage of every single one we made. Never did anyone see the world through such malicious eyes.'

'Is it my fault if the world does not bear looking at?'

'You have sawn off the branch you were sitting on.'

'The tree was rotten, Mme Arthème.'

Then silence falls between them and their thoughts drift even further away. Mme Arthème makes a restless movement. But it is Dod who speaks:

'You see, I would have liked to be a lecturer at some university in the North. I would have spent my sabbatical year travelling. To take up your metaphor, I have never sawn off any branch. All my life I have had this sensation of falling. For that reason I would have liked at last to move horizontally, across ancient Europe, mysterious Asia and America with its vast landscapes and huge rivers, under a wider sky.... I would have visited museums and fished - and why not? - for salmon in the Salmon River. Once you have a permit you have the right, so I've discovered to catch two salmon a year. More than enough. None of which does anything to diminish my gratitude to you for having attempted to arrest my fall and for having given me tonight this opportunity of exchanging one or two ideas with you. '

'When I have left this room who will you cry out to for help like a weepy little boy who's afraid of the dark?'

'You, of course. But you won't hear me. '

Mme Arthème gives a nod, her face beginning to soften with the marks of fatigue left by a long and strenuous day. She wraps her big grey cloak more tightly around her.

Dod cannot help saying: 'I fear your opinion of Mme Luffergal is, if you'll forgive my pointing this out to you, somewhat ill-considered. '

'A fine woman. I have left her very precise instructions regarding you. Shall I turn out the light?'

'The light of this lamp is mellow and the switch in any case within my reach. '

'I didn't want to leave without saying good-bye to you. '

'I shall miss your diligent and solicitous attentions. '

The stern face turns away and in a moment Dod is aware only of her rapid, dwindling foot-steps, their ancient echo ringing down the long dark dormitories of his boyhood.

A LETTER FROM OLIVIER

High Wycombe, Thursday

Dear old Dod,
We're getting married. After all the doubts and hesi-
tations and torments.... What a heap of nonsense! I
believe I can still be happy yet. With her I will be. It
was decided yesterday afternoon. Officially, that is,
because our decision had already been taken in Rome
after she joined me there. I didn't have time to see
you after returning from Italy. In any case I didn't
particularly want to. I'm sorry. I would have felt
ridiculous. In fact to put it bluntly I was scared of
your... corrosive influence. Your terrifying scepticism.
And yet you're the first to suffer its effects. I've been
hearing bad news about your health. However, I hope
and assume it's no more than one of those dry runs
you're in the habit of taking. A few days from now I'll
be in Sarmes. With her. She's enrolling at the
University. I've got another year to do as you know.
The wedding will be in London at the end of the year.
See you soon. You're going to feel you have a double
friend beside you now. I know you'll like her. And at
the bottom of your heart you know perfectly well: life
isn't so terrible. See you soon.

Olivier.

It was nine o'clock in the evening. A sound like a
surging crowd was rising from the street but Dod, his
mind dulled and his senses numb, was only vaguely
aware of it. A firework went off, making him jump.
Then he heard what sounded like a brass band approaching
He glanced towards the bathroom. Amalia was getting
washed and dressed preparatory to leaving for the
Lovely Lady. The noise beneath the window intensified
and more firewords exploded. Dod threw back the
covers and swung his legs out of the bed he had not
left for the last two days. Hardly was he on his feet
than he had to sit down again. His legs felt curiously
wobbly. He wondered whether he was still suffering
the effects of the attack that had prostrated him back
there in that studio.... He shivered. He was completely naked. His clothes were still scattered over
the armchair; no one had thought to tidy them away or
even fold them up. With awkward, clumsy gestures -
things kept slipping out of his hands - staggering slightly,
biting back a dizzy nausea that seemed to come from
standing up, he got himself dressed. The brass band,
very close now, blared out a discordant travesty of a
fanfare to the accompaniment of shouts, bursts of song,
exclamations and applause. Dod drew back the double
curtains and opened the window. A mocking ovation
greeted him. He was on the point of stepping back
when he realized it was not him they were acclaiming -
out in that narrow and perhaps familiar street which
looked like most of the streets in the harbour district

188

but which he was seeing for the first time from Amalia's room - amid the smell of burnt gunpowder, the blaze of lights - not him they were acclaiming, that excited, yelling crowd, young people for the most part, with here and there a grotesque mask - no, that excited, gesticulating crowd was parting before the improbable-sounding brass band which had announced its presence so far in advance, its frightful racket even so giving no hint of its actual appearance, the musicians being got up in gawdy stage-props as burlesque Mexicans, Bretons, Bavarians, Russians - with a few throw-outs from Italian opera too - some of them blowing bugles, others bashing drums with as much energy as they had contempt for the beat - yet others carrying torches whose flickering flames threw giant shadows on the walls for one second of magnificence before a puff of wind or the jerk of an arm provoked their pitiful collapse.

Dod turned to find Amalia watching him. She did not answer his question immediately and he became impatient: 'Will you kindly tell me what all that's in aid of?'

She shrugged.

'Have you forgotten today's the seventh centenary of the founding of the University? There were big ceremonies this morning with cabinet ministers, all the professors.... Now comes the fun. That's your student friends making all that row.'

Dod had indeed forgotten. He passed a hand over his face. Had he lost all notion of time? Up until a few days before - when, though - making all those plans with his friends for this famous evening, this longed-for celebration.... What had happened to his fierce appetite for pleasure? His gay abandon? Keeping a tight grip on the window-sill to stop himself falling he leaned out over the street once more, and this time spotted Kell. Dressed in a harlequin costume though with his head bare he was bringing up the rear of the

procession, beating with huge conviction and an air of
hilarity on the bass drum borne along before him almost
at ground-level...and Dod recognized the dwarf Basal,
crushed beneath his burden, struggling to keep his head
up, twisting it to one side and staring skywards with a
tortured expression on his face. His eyes looked straight
into Dod's. He appeared not to recognize him. But Dod
did. Dod recognized him, and he was suddenly struck
by a revelation: that face, deformed as if by the pressure
of some monstrous thumb, that face of a carnival Christ
was the face of the last arcanum of the tarot pack, the
face of the Fool, ridiculous, pitiful, a mastiff snapping
at his heels - and, over and above all physical resemblance, that face was also his own.

Dod turned abruptly from the window. Amalia had
not moved.

'I'm going back to her,' he said.

'No.'

'I want to see her again.'

'No, it's too late. She's left for London. This
evening....'

She hesitated. She was looking at him with a thoughtful troubled expression which betrayed a rare absence
of her usual resolution, as if she were weighing in
some mysterious balance a for and against that were
both equally unknowable. But soon all that was buried
beneath an expression of utter indifference.

'She hasn't quite gone, not yet,' she said. 'She'll
be on the boat by now but it doesn't sail for another
half-hour. It's the Phoenix, moored at the Quai Saint-
Paul. You may just catch her.'

Later, at Dr. Nauser's clinic, in the mists where Mme
Artheme's injections kept him floating, Dod imagined
he really had gone dashing off in pursuit of Mary Seymour
through the crowds which that evening clogged the maze
of little streets round the harbour, and that he had run
and run, bumping into figures in fancy dress, their

190

masked faces sneering derisively at him from all
sides.... Then, coming out onto the quay where the
Phoenix towered up only a few yards ahead of him, he
had felt the wind off the sea in his face and in the same
instant sea and sky had started spinning madly, the
ground had given abruptly beneath his feet, he had felt
a kind of quick, powerful suction from below.... And
then, too, he thought it was just before they took him
away, as the howl of the siren dragged on and on - was
it the siren of the ambulance or of the ship? - there,
floating above him for a moment like a sarcastic mask,
was the face of Dr. Nauser; but Dr. Nauser was nodding
his head and saying - how could one disbelieve him? -
Dr. Nauser was saying that the young man had been
brought to him several months previously by his parents,
that he had left the clinic prematurely, that he had
found him lying on the floor of Amalia's room, a childhood friend, don't you know, and a fine person in spite
of everything, who had rung him up and asked him to
come and take this blinking nuisance off her hands,
referring to his patient, now finally recovered.

Dod, his eyes open, is listening to old Lousine. How busy she is this morning. How she's pottering about. And the sluggish October dawn not even blanching the window yet.... Now to one side, now to the other, her walking-stick darting with little quick taps across the ceiling, now stopping, now setting off again, obstinately, indefatigably. Never as early as this before. Nor for so long. What are these extraordinary preparations in aid of? A journey, perhaps? He smiles at the idea. Perhaps they'll be leaving together. He smiles again at this fresh idea. Perhaps she's packing her little bags. Dod derives from this what amusement he can. He, at any rate, is ready. Suddenly alert to the sound of the lift coming up.... For him? The ambulance... already? But the lift stops two or three floors below. And the silence returns, broken only by the tapping of old Lousine's walking-stick, now becoming busier and busier. And now she's opening her door.

The night is doing away with itself the way the man who has come to his senses one day turns his back on the schemes of childhood, and the room, as it is drained of shadow, becomes filled with fog, its shape uncertain, lending itself once again to every complaisance. And as the lift starts off again and continues without stopping up to the floor above, and goes back down with someone he will never see, Dod closes his eyes, still smiling sighs, is at peace, notes that noises now resound differently, in another, different space, and says to himself that it will in any case be too late, that when they come, if they ever do come, all they will find will be an empty room.